SMUGGL
SMUGGL

Trevor May

RIGGING OUT A SMUGGLER.

SHIRE PUBLICATIONS

Published by Shire Publications, part of
Bloomsbury Publishing Plc.
PO Box 883, Oxford, OX1 9PL, UK
1385 Broadway, 5th Floor, New York, NY 10018, USA
Email: shire@shirebooks.co.uk   www.shirebooks.co.uk

Transferred to digital print on demand 2018

First published 2014
1st impression 2014

Printed and bound by PrintOnDemand-Worldwide.com,
Peterborough, UK

A CIP catalogue record for this book is available from the
British Library.

Shire Library 713   ISBN-13: 978 0 74781 207 4
PDF eBook ISBN: 978 1 78442 000 0
ePub ISBN: 978 0 74781 540 2

Trevor May has asserted his right under the Copyright,
Designs and Patents Act, 1988, to be identified as the
author of this book.

Designed by Tony Truscott Designs, Sussex, UK
Typeset in Perpetua and Gill Sans.

COVER IMAGE
Cover design by Peter Ashley. Front cover: *The Onslaught
of the Smugglers*, c. 1837 (oil on canvas), Louis Eugene
Gabriel Isabey (1803–86) (courtesy of Musée de la
Chartreuse, Douai, France / Giraudon / The Bridgeman
Art Library). Back cover: A smuggler's lantern, from an
Ogden's cigarette card, collection of Peter Ashley.

TITLE PAGE IMAGE
Rigging out a Smuggler, a caricature by Thomas
Rowlandson, engraved by Thomas Tegg. A seaman loads
a woman with contraband, including tea, otto (oil) of
roses and 'coniac'. These will be covered by her outer
clothing. Although such methods of concealment were not
unknown to the small-scale operator, much smuggling was
on an industrial scale.

CONTENTS PAGE IMAGE
Greenock Custom House, painted by Robert Salmon
in 1820. A steam vessel and a variety of sailing ships
contribute to this busy scene on the River Clyde.

ACKNOWLEDGEMENTS
Illustrations are acknowledged as follows:
Susan Bailey, page 54 (top); Brian Batters, page 35; The
Bridgeman Art Library / The Advertising Archives, page 70;
Cornish Tea Company, page 7 (top); Edinburgh College
of Art Cast Collection, The University of Edinburgh,
Photograph by John K. McGregor, page 29; Steve Harris,
page 27 (bottom); Government Art Collection, page 37
(bottom); Hidden Britain (http://www.hiddenbritainse.
org.uk), page 6 (top), 59 (bottom); Jon Holland, page 12
(top); Lewiscollard.com, page 26; Courtesy of the Lewis
Walpole Library, Yale University, pages 7 (bottom), 16, 48
(top), 61, 66 (top and bottom); Littlehampton Museum,
pages 46, 47; Bill McKenzie / Scottish Viewpoint, page
57; Merseyside Maritime Museum, pages 45 (top), 67;
McLean Museum and Art Gallery, Greenock, contents
page; National Maritime Museum, title page and pages
18, 25, 30, 36 (bottom), 38, 41, 42, 50, 51; Old Town
Museum, Hastings, page 24 (right); Chris Petty, page
44 (top); The Printing Historical Society, 17 (bottom);
Chris Rudge, page 71 (top); Nick Scott, page 45 (bottom);
N. R. Thomason, page 71 (bottom); Toy Theatre Gallery,
Glasgow, 9 (top); Mark Twyning, page 54 (bottom);
Mick Walsh, page 58; Steve Wassell, page 12 (bottom).

DEDICATION
For my grandsons: Angus May, Felix May and Harry Brown.

Shire Publications is supporting the Woodland Trust, the UK's leading woodland conservation charity, by funding the dedication of trees.

CONTENTS

SMUGGLER

HEROES AND VILLAINS

In 2008 representatives of civic and business interests in Hawkhurst, Kent, came together to seek ways of boosting tourism and trade in the village, a community of some 4,400 inhabitants. The resulting Hawkhurst Community Partnership took professional marketing advice and came up with its first major project: the setting up of the Hawkhurst Gang Smugglers' Trail, incorporating sites in the village and surrounding area associated with one of the most vicious criminal gangs of the eighteenth century. The trail was judged a great success. The lesson was well learnt that smugglers are good for business.

Searching for the word 'smuggler' in any form of directory will produce scores of businesses that benefit from association with a locality's smuggling past. Beyond the expected inns and public houses, they include restaurants and tea rooms, holiday cottages, gift shops – even trades as tangential as property maintenance. Responding to the public fascination with this subject is entirely pragmatic; and, indeed, there is nothing new in this.

In the eighteenth and early nineteenth centuries so many people gained advantage from smuggling that it was all too easy to divorce this from any moral consideration. In September 1891 the *Royal Cornwall Gazette* related the story of a London curate visiting an elderly woman in a stuffy backroom of a house in the capital. She told him that she had been born in Cornwall, and in her younger days had 'made a bit of money' through the smuggling activities of her husband, who was a petty officer on a naval packet ship. In reply to the curate's expression of shock, she replied, 'Well you see, sir, there is no harm in it down to Cornwall; of course, up here it's different.' With a touch of irony, the article categorised this 'topographical morality' as 'altogether charming'. Although it may have been charming, it was probably not a true reflection. Attitudes towards smuggling were similar throughout the kingdom.

Smuggling took place in every coastal region of Great Britain, with the port of London being one of the worst affected areas. The practice found its

Opposite:
The Smuggler, by G. P. R. James. First published in 1845, James wrote of the book that it presented 'a correct picture of Kent … some eighty or ninety years ago'. The cover shown here is from a cheap 'yellowback' edition printed in 1872; examples of the latter were very popular with railway travellers.

5

A smuggler re-enactor holds one of the interpretation boards for the Hawkhurst Gang Smugglers' Trail, promoted by the Hawkhurst Community Partnership in Kent.

supporters there as elsewhere; indeed, few took a firm moral stand against smuggling. One who did so was John Wesley. In his pamphlet of 1767, *A Word to a Smuggler*, Wesley directed his ethical concerns to all who benefited from smuggling. He cast his net widely. There were, he argued, four kinds of smuggler: firstly, those who imported run (smuggled) goods; secondly, sea captains and others who imported goods without paying the duty that the law required; thirdly, those who sold goods on which duty had not been paid; and fourthly, 'those who buy tea, liquors, linen, handkerchiefs, or anything else which has not paid duty'. He reserved his most scathing remarks for the last group, countering such common defences as 'I did not know that the goods were smuggled', 'I only buy a little brandy or tea now and then, just for my own use', and 'If I could get what has paid duty, I am not able to pay the price of it; and I cannot live without it.' Wesley poured particular scorn on the last example. 'You can live without it,' he raged, 'as well as your grandmother did.' He developed such a passionate hatred for tea, much of which was smuggled, that he gave up drinking it. His example, however, was not followed by many.

Nine years after Wesley took his high ethical stand the philosopher Adam Smith, in his 1776 book *The Wealth of Nations*, expressed a less moralistic line.

> The smuggler, he said, was a person who, though no doubt highly blameable for violating the laws of his country, is frequently incapable of violating

Ye Olde Smugglers Inne, in the village of Alfriston, Sussex, was formerly known as Market Cross House. It was the home of Stanton Collins, a butcher and leader of a local gang of smugglers. In 1831 he was charged with theft, and sentenced to transportation for seven years.

those of natural justice, and would have been, in every respect, an excellent citizen had not the laws of his country made that a crime which nature never meant to be so ... Not many people are scrupulous about smuggling when, without perjury, they can find any easy and safe opportunity of doing so ... By this indulgence of the public, the smuggler is often encouraged to continue a trade which he is thus taught to consider as in some measure innocent.

The essayist Charles Lamb (1775–1834) was even more sympathetic. 'I like the smuggler,' he said, 'he is the only honest thief. He robs nothing but the Revenue, an abstraction I never greatly cared about.' Lamb, it should be added, was for over thirty years a clerk in the accounting department of the East India Company, while Adam Smith held the post of Commissioner of Customs in Edinburgh between 1778 and his death in 1790.

An enterprising tea company in Cornwall is one of many businesses taking commercial advantage of a public fascination with smuggling.

Although Lamb may have liked the smuggler, few people today would profess any admiration for the contemporary practitioner. The drug smuggler, the international trader in endangered species, and the people trafficker are widely regarded as enemies of society rather than popular heroes. Yet in the period since Lamb wrote, the smugglers of yesteryear have become melodramatic and romanticised figures, whose virtues and

GENUINE TEA COMPANY

A group of working people (including a coalman) drink tea at a street stall in this 1825 print. The title *Genuine Tea Company* is no doubt an ironic comment on the fact that much tea was adulterated. Used tea leaves might be dried and cut with 'smouch', a mixture of ash leaves and sheep dung.

(to a lesser extent) villainies have been exaggerated. This transformation began in the early nineteenth century, if not before. The exploits of the smuggler were represented in the widest range of cultural forms, including the folk ballad, the theatre, painting, poetry and novel, and later the cinema.

In the early part of the nineteenth century many popular ballads were printed as broadsides (on a large single-sided sheet). A number of these related to smuggling, including 'The Female Smuggler', 'The Exciseman', and, most notably, 'Will Watch, the Bold Smuggler'. In the latter Will promises his love, Susan, that after one final foray he will give up

An early twentieth-century depiction of Will Watch by the illustrator Veronica Whall. It appeared in *Ships, Sea Songs and Shanties* by W. B. Whall, published in 1913. The dashing young smuggler made a perfect romantic hero – in song, if not always in reality.

Smugglers resting up in a ruined hut. This colourful illustration by N. M. Price is from an 1890s edition of Sir Walter Scott's novel, *Guy Mannering*.

smuggling and will settle down. However, the revenue men catch up with him and he is shot. His body is buried on the beach, according to his wishes. The ballad was popular on both sides of the Atlantic; in 1842 Charles Dickens saw a copy posted on the wall of a low tavern in New York's notorious Five Points district. Theatrical versions of Will Watch's tale were followed by numerous stage melodramas in which smugglers featured.

Other representations of the smuggler came directly into the home through the novel and poetry. This included both

popular literature (so ephemeral that it is now hard to trace) and works of greater literary merit. Although G. P. R. James was the author of over one hundred works, including *The Smuggler* (1845), few of these are read today. James had been recommended to take up writing as a profession by Sir Walter Scott, whose *Guy Mannering* (1815) included smuggling as a major theme. Scott's character of Dirk Hatteraik, a Dutch smuggler operating between Holland and Scotland, was allegedly based on Captain Jack Yawkins, a noted Scottish smuggler.

Likewise, several of Captain Frederick Marryat's stories touch upon smuggling, including *The Pirate and the Three Cutters* (1836). Marryat, a naval officer, had commanded the revenue cutter *Rosario* in the early 1820s; the ship makes an appearance as one of the three referred to in the title. Marryat's book, however, largely ignores the *Rosario*, and what he does say of it is disparaging. It is the smugglers' cutter that takes centre stage, with its captain Jack Pickersgill ('the *beau idéal* of a handsome sailor') eventually winning the hand of a fair lady. Thomas Hardy wrote of smuggling, and his romance *The Distracted Preacher*, first published in *Wessex Tales* in 1888, gives a vivid account of the struggle between smugglers and preventive men (those involved in guarding the coastline and preventing smuggling).

The fascination with smuggling continued into the twentieth century.

A sheet of characters for the two-act drama *The Smuggler*, written for the toy theatre and published in Webb's Junior Drama series. These sheets can be difficult to date as they were frequently reprinted. Robert Louis Stevenson had a great enthusiasm for the toy theatre and recalled being entranced by this play as a child.

The cover of a 1915 American edition of *Dr. Syn: a Smuggler Tale of the Romney Marsh*, the first of Russell Thorndike's popular smuggling novels.

'Brandy for the Parson, 'Baccy for the Clerk …'. Rudyard Kipling's poem 'A Smuggler's Song' was included in his collection *Puck of Pook's Hill* in 1906. Kipling was then living at Burwash in East Sussex, formerly a notorious smuggling region. This illustration by Paul Hardy was inspired by the poem and appeared in Charles G. Harper's *The Smugglers*, published in 1909. Although the image is benign, Kipling's poem has an altogether darker tone.

Robert Stephen Hawker (1803–75) was from 1834 until his death the vicar of Morwenstow, on the north Cornish coast. An eccentric character with wide literary and antiquarian interests, Hawker wrote much about smuggling. His biographer C. E. Byles observed: 'There is an element of fiction in Hawker's biographical studies. He never lets facts, or the absence of them, stand in the way of his imagination.' The same may be said of numerous others who wrote about smuggling.

In 1915 Russell Thorndike published *Dr. Syn: a Smuggler Tale of the Romney Marsh*, featuring the smuggling hero the Reverend Doctor Christopher Syn. A further six volumes followed, the last being *The Shadow of Dr. Syn*, which appeared in 1944. Moreover, there were many film and television adaptations of the Dr. Syn books.

Early cinema had quickly embraced the subject of smuggling. Between 1904 and the end of the First World War at least eight British films on a smuggling theme had appeared, and the cinema retained its enthusiasm for the subject in subsequent decades. Perhaps the most famous example is the 1949 film *Whisky Galore!* This was based on Sir Compton Mackenzie's novel, which had been published two years previously. *Whisky Galore!* was based on fact, namely the wrecking of the SS *Politician* off the Hebridean island of Eriskay in February 1941. A large part of the cargo of 24,000 tons of spirits (mainly whisky) was 'spirited away' by the islanders. So legendary did this story become that in November 1987 eight bottles of so-called 'Polly' whisky came up for auction in Edinburgh, where they realised a total of £4,000.

In truth, *Whisky Galore!* is a tale of wrecking (the taking of goods and material from a wrecked ship) rather than smuggling. The use of false lights, to entice ships onto rocks so that they would break up and might be plundered, is often associated with Cornwall, but it is hard to find hard evidence relating to this practice. The same applies to smuggling in general. Successful smugglers left no trail. Historians work from hard evidence, and this often means they focus on those who produce it – usually the authorities and those with power. Ambivalent views towards smuggling persist because so much presumed knowledge derives from folk memory and legend. If an accurate account is to be provided, the researcher must proceed with caution.

THE NATURE OF SMUGGLING

SMUGGLING has existed ever since governments first attempted to control trade across their borders. Although it is often understood as an attempt to evade duties or taxes that the legislature has placed upon the *importation* of certain classes of goods, smuggling is a much broader phenomenon than this. It may apply to attempts to evade export regulations, for example, or trade in certain prohibited goods, such as weapons or drugs. People may be smuggled across frontiers (or 'trafficked' if the movement is without their consent). At one end of the spectrum smuggling may be a highly organised criminal activity, or what some describe as 'the smuggling industry'; at the other it may consist simply of a sailor or passenger trying to slip something for personal use past the authorities.

Consideration must also be given to attempts to evade regulations relating to internal trade. Taxes on this are classified as excise duties. At one time, compliance was enforced by excise officers, while international trade was policed by customs officers; latterly, the two revenue services have been merged into one.

While the collection of revenue was the key role of the Customs service, officers were also assigned other tasks. They acted as receivers of wrecks, with responsibility to give assistance to vessels in distress, and to secure and protect salvaged cargo. In addition, the Quarantine Act of 1710 set out procedures that customs officers were required to enforce. These included

Seaford Martello tower is at the southern end of a chain of 103 coastal towers built between Aldeburgh in Suffolk and Eastbourne in Sussex in the period 1805–12. Designed as defensive forts against French invasion, after 1815 they took on a new function when they became coastguard stations in the war against smuggling.

the administration of the quarantine oath. Sworn by a ship's master, this oath declared his vessel to be free of infectious disease. For this purpose, a Bible (encased in an iron or copper container) was passed from the customs boat on the end of a boathook or line. After the oath had been sworn, the enclosed Bible was thrown back in the water, the belief being that towing it through salt water would remove any trace of infection. Of course, the criminal mind can turn most things to its advantage. In January 1832 – at the height of a cholera scare – the *Royal Cornwall Gazette* reported the case of a vessel, 'having the appearance of a large foreign fishing smack', lying off the county's east coast. From its topmast it carried the flag signalling 'contagious disease on board'. It aroused no particular suspicion, and no boat went anywhere near it. At night, however, the vessel landed a valuable cargo of contraband on the beach

Smugglers Cott restaurant in Polperro, Cornwall, occupies a house built in the early fifteenth century. Remains of a tunnel leading to the quayside may indicate that it was once used by smugglers.

before making a hasty retreat.

In addition to raising revenue, control of exports and imports was seen as a vital means of encouraging domestic manufacture. For example, in 1463 the Company of Comb Makers had persuaded Parliament to pass an Act prohibiting the importation of all foreign combs (other than from Ireland). Nearly three centuries later, in July 1750, the Commissioners of Customs were reminding their officers in all ports that the law still applied

The only certainty about Culver Hole, near Port Eynon on the Gower Peninsula, derives from its name. Given that 'culver' is an archaic name for a dove or pigeon, the cave was very likely used in the medieval period to trap birds for food. The much later stonework is more difficult to account for. Local lore has it that this was a smugglers' lair.

and was to be strictly enforced. In terms of its national importance, a far more significant industry was that of wool production. In this case the perceived need was to deny foreign manufacturers (especially in Flanders) access to the English raw material. In an attempt to tighten controls, from 1353 certain 'staple towns' were designated as the sole ports through which wool might be legally exported. This did not stop the illegal export of wool which, according to one estimate, amounted to 120,000 packs annually. The smugglers were known as owlers, probably because their activities were largely confined to night-time; another, less likely explanation is that the word is a corruption of 'woolers'. The illegal export of wool was concentrated on the Kent and Sussex coast. In 1690 a force of mounted customs officers was established; however, with only eight of them to patrol the length of the Kent coast, their effectiveness was negligible.

In an attempt to maintain its technical lead in textile manufacturing, Parliament passed a series of Acts between 1719 and 1799 designed to prohibit the emigration of artisans and the export of machinery. Although the provisions relating to emigration were repealed in 1825, those on the export of machinery lasted until 1843. The laws did not succeed, and much technology was smuggled abroad. This cotton machinery is at the Helmshore Mills Textile Museum in Lancashire.

Before the Industrial Revolution of the mid eighteenth century, much of Britain's industrial power was located in the southern half of England. The counties that are now more closely associated with farming and tourism once echoed to the sounds of furnace and loom. In Tudor and Stuart times the Weald of Kent and Sussex was the main iron-producing region in Britain. There were well over one hundred furnaces by the late sixteenth century, all dependent on local sources of ironstone, and charcoal from the abundant Wealden woodland. From the mid seventeenth century, industry concentrated on the casting of cannon, the majority of domestic production being found here until about 1770. By that time the Wealden iron industry was suffering decline; local sources of charcoal were becoming exhausted, and there was fierce competition from regions where coal supplies enabled coke furnaces to be used. Other employment had to be found, and to many people smuggling proved an attractive alternative.

In Devon and Cornwall, another region with a solid reputation for smuggling, the illegal export of tin and copper was a major issue with which the authorities had to contend. The Duchy of Cornwall had acquired the right to purchase, at a fixed rate, all tin offered for sale. Until 1838 tin had to be taken to stannary towns, where the ingots were weighed and stamped

Caves at Ladram Bay, between Budleigh Salterton and Sidmouth, on the south coast of Devon. A lack of hard evidence adds to the romance of smuggling. Many beaches around Britain's coast are suitable for landing smuggled goods, and some caves were certainly used by smugglers, if only as temporary hiding places. Legend and folk tales flourish in such circumstances.

prior to sale. Among the noted stannary towns, which changed over time, were Totnes, Tavistock, Saltash and Lostwithiel. Alongside this legal trade many unstamped ingots of tin and copper were smuggled abroad. It has been estimated that, at certain key points in time, as much as three-quarters of all tin leaving Cornwall was smuggled. Despite the hazardous conditions in which they toiled, tinners were not well paid; in the middle of the eighteenth century they could expect to earn no more than 16 to 21*s.* (shillings) per month. It is little wonder that smuggling should prove an attractive proposition. Those who did not directly participate in smuggling would nevertheless provide a ready market for cheap, smuggled spirits.

In 1749, Harry Carter, brother of John Carter, the so-called 'King of Prussia', was born at Breage, near Helston in west Cornwall. His father was a miner, with a small rented farm. He worked in local tin mines until he was seventeen when, in what he describes almost as a career move, he 'went with [his] two oldest brothers to Porthleah or the King's Cove afishing and smuggling.' The combination of fishing and smuggling was a popular form of diversification. Each activity required a high standard of seamanship and knowledge of coastal waters, while the same vessel could be used for either purpose.

The authorities had great difficulty in distinguishing small boats used for legitimate and illegal activities. One of the first things preventive men did when boarding a boat allegedly engaged in fishing was to feel the nets; if they were dry, there was an assumption that the crew were up to no good. Boats were required to be licensed, and there were restrictions on dimensions, the number of oars and the size of the crew. The name of the owner and the port from which the boat operated had to be painted on it; furthermore, from 1832 all boats including fishing boats were to be painted black. Although this might seem counter-intuitive, it helped make them more visible at night.

Newhaven fishermen and fishwives depicted in an 1862 engraving from the *Illustrated London News*. Many fishermen engaged in smuggling, on both a small and large scale. Unless previously known to the authorities, it proved impossible to distinguish the legitimate worker from the law breaker.

Then, as now, fishermen faced foreign competition, and the Dutch developed a trade with the London market, which West Country fishermen found harder to exploit. A correspondent in the *Royal Cornwall Gazette* of 20 April 1822 bewailed the lack of enterprise of local fishermen and blamed the taste that had been acquired for smuggling: 'The evil I believe is to be traced to an insatiable but misplaced love of gain, and the fixed habits of the veteran Smuggler, who has ruined the morals of his rising family.'

Farmers complained in a similar way of the corrupting influence of smuggling on their labour force. David Phillipson (see *Further reading*) quotes the following lament from a letter in the *Gentleman's Magazine* of September 1735: 'In several parts of Kent the farmers are obliged to raise wages, and yet are distressed for want of hands to get in their harvest, which is attributed to the great numbers who employ themselves in smuggling along the coast.' The farmers conveniently forgot who provided them with their cheap spirits and tea.

The distressingly low wages of agricultural labourers made indulging in smuggling an attractive proposition. Reporting on the agriculture of Sussex in 1813, Arthur Young noted that general farm labourers earned from 16 to 18*d*. (pence) a day. By contrast, for merely conveying goods from the smuggling vessel to the shore, a man could earn 2*s*. 7*d*. a night. It is hardly surprising that with their low wages, abysmal housing and poor diet, many farm workers would have regarded smuggling (like poaching) as a form of social protest, as well as a way of putting food on the table. A minor footnote to history supports this view. On Saturday 15 March 1834 the Western Circuit Assizes commenced at Dorchester, with sixty-two names on the list of prisoners ordered for trial. History remembers six of them – the so-called Tolpuddle Martyrs, who were charged with administering unlawful

I don't understand what they mean by they Debates. coust this Jell. Robins?

Why I take it it means this, th'min ith Parliament up at Lunnon make sham quarrels; and then grine at us folk ith country for believen um to be in Arnest!!

Oh Featherjuby theel be just like Dr Solomon with folks that swallows his balm of Quillad!

A SHREWED GUESS or the Farmers definition of Parliamentary Debates

"He laughs of him in a fair log
O you miskine him; Else on humble one
The fawning joy of boundaries with yd a"

In this print of 1813 a farmer and his wife express scant regard for politicians. Although their surroundings are plain, the cups and the tankard show that she has her tea, and he has his beer (with, no doubt, some brandy tucked away). While many farmers complained of the impact of smuggling on their labour force, they were grateful to make gains from the trade.

oaths at a meeting to organise a union of farm workers. Less well known is that the list also included four poachers and, significantly, six smugglers.

Clearly, many of the labouring poor did not regard smuggling as criminal. Moreover, large numbers in the middle and upper classes found themselves acquiescing in this view, if only because so many of them were beneficiaries of smuggling. 'Yorkshire George' Watson was a smuggler hanged for murder on 5 July 1736 – allegedly the only smuggler to suffer that fate at Tyburn 'for many years'. Although it was said that he 'dyed without showing any Concern', the chaplain of Newgate prison made use of the prisoner's last words from the scaffold (as was commonplace) to make a broader point:

[Watson] protested that he was very well satisfied with the Justice of that Law by [which] he died, and of all the Laws against Smuggling; but he said, it were to be wished that People of Estates and Distinction, who had all the Opportunities of knowing the Law they could desire, and at the same Time under no Temptation to break them, would curb their Inclinations for run and prohibited Goods, and not buy for the Sake of some Abatement of Price, or Beauty in the Commodity, Teas or Silks tinctured with the Blood of poor Men: It lay in their Power he said in a great Measure, to repress this

Evil, for Smuglers [sic] like Thieves, would no longer have any Desire to sin, when through Want of Receivers, all Hopes of Profit were taken away; for as he observed, what Likelihood can there be of suppressing Smugglers, when hardly one Gentleman in five, but has a run Handkerchief in his Pocket, and while the best Families in the Kingdom make no Scruple of drinking their Tea, provided they can have it safely and two Shillings in a Pound under Price. (*The Proceedings of the Old Bailey, 1674–1913*)

Parliament found it very difficult to repress the perceived evil of smuggling, because duties were such an important element in the national finances. War was endemic throughout the eighteenth century, and war was expensive. It swallowed up the public finances; between 75 and 85 per cent of annual public expenditure went on the army and the navy or on servicing the national debt which, by the start of the war with France in 1793, had reached nearly £293 million (around £13.7 billion in today's terms). With customs duties providing around a fifth of public revenues throughout the eighteenth century, it was difficult for the government to respond to those who claimed that reducing duties would diminish smuggling. Instead, and following the spirit of the times, the government passed ever more restrictive legislation and imposed more draconian punishments.

A cartoon from *Punch,* showing the home of a rick-burner. Smuggling, like poaching and rick-burning, has been interpreted as a form of social protest, whereby those with little or no political power could get back at those they considered to be their oppressors.

A printer's stock block for a tea advertisement. The empty speech bubble is designed to facilitate the insertion of a local supplier's name. Legitimate tea dealers needed to advertise, and the irony is that probably only a few tea drinkers knew where their tea came from. Much was smuggled.

ENFORCING THE LAW

THE AGENCIES with responsibility for enforcing the law and bringing miscreants to justice were numerous. At different times in the eighteenth and nineteenth centuries they included the Customs service, the Excise, the Coastguard and the Coastal Blockade service, the navy, the army and militia, and the police. There were ample opportunities for rivalry between these departments, and disputes were commonplace.

The Customs service on a national scale can be traced back to around 1203. At that time the collection of all customs dues was removed from local control and devolved to a system administered by the Exchequer. To improve accountability, a system of checks and balances was established. At each port a collector was appointed, with the responsibility of collecting duties and receiving payment. A second official, the comptroller, kept a second set of accounts, although no money passed through his hands. Both these sets of accounts were then forwarded to the Exchequer in London. Thirdly, a searcher was appointed; in early times his duty was to examine imported and exported goods and to ensure that all duties had been paid, but by the eighteenth century his role was confined to exports.

In 1671 a Board of Commissioners of Customs was established by Charles II. The commissioners issued orders and regulations to the officers at the outports (those beyond London), with whom they maintained a steady correspondence. By 1783 the board was answering some 9,000 letters a year from local officers. Although much was subsequently destroyed by fire, this correspondence provides a key source for the history of smuggling.

The hands-on job of preventing smuggling was given to the Landguard and Waterguard services. The Landguard consisted of landwaiters, who supervised the unloading of ships from foreign ports, and riding officers, who were first appointed in 1698 to combat owling, and continued to be employed until 1821. Riding officers had the unenviable task of patrolling

Opposite:
In this 1830 lithograph by William Heath, a pretty maid encounters a revenue officer. His challenge, 'Why Polly, you an't on the smuggling take, I hope', seems more flirtatious than hostile. The contrast in sentiment with the illustration on page 21 is striking.

Dragoons often resented being employed to quell smuggling, partly because officers showed a reluctance to share rewards and prize money with their men.

There had been a Custom House in Lower Thames Street, London, since the fourteenth century. Destroyed in the Great Fire of 1666, it was rebuilt by Sir Christopher Wren, only to be burned down again in 1714. Its successor (shown here) was built between 1717 and 1725. In its turn, this building burned down in 1818. This series of fires destroyed many records relating to customs administration and smuggling.

the coast on the lookout for any signs of smuggling activity. The work was by its nature lonely, and the sense of isolation was made worse by the indifference or active resentment of much of the local population. The pay was poor — averaging around £40 or so a year — and out of it the officer had to provide and maintain a horse. Benjamin Elliot, a riding officer based at Marazion in Cornwall in 1748, had a run of bad luck; either that, or he was a poor judge of horses. The first mount he purchased died soon afterwards; the second turned vicious and had to be sold at a loss; the third went blind; and a fourth died after only a year's service.

A riding officer was expected to be out in all weathers, and had to patrol a stretch of coastline that was officially four miles, but often much longer. He was also empowered to keep watch up to ten miles inland. Many died as a result of violence, or in suspicious circumstances. Such was the fate of John Hurley, the riding officer at Branscombe, Devon. In August 1755 he was patrolling the cliffs near Seaton when he came across a number of women (presumed to have been wives of members of a smuggling gang from the village of Beer). The women were making fires at the cliff edge as a signal to an incoming smuggling vessel. Somehow Hurley fell over the cliff and was killed. At the subsequent inquest the women swore on oath that

he had tumbled while running from one fire to another in order to extinguish them. He may, of course, have been pushed; however, with no other witnesses the coroner had no choice but to record a verdict of accidental death. A few years earlier, in the winter of 1739/40, Thomas Carswell, a revenue officer stationed at Rye, East Sussex, was murdered by members of the Hawkhurst Gang while he was escorting back to Hastings a wagonload of tea that had been landed earlier at Bulverhythe. A corporal and three dragoons who were with him were badly wounded. Following this incident, orders were issued that revenue officers at Rye had to have an adequate military escort with them when they set out to make a seizure.

THE "PREVENTIVE" WATER-GUARD OR COASTGUARD.
A CARICATURE OF 1833.

In this caricature of 1833, a feisty woman challenges a coastguard: 'I'll lay you a crown that you can't prewent me from giving you a good dab on the chops.' He carries his cutlass under his arm as casually as if he were going for an afternoon stroll. Many coastguards were said to be elderly and infirm. Compare this with the image on page 18.

Dragoons cut down fleeing smugglers – an illustration by Paul Hardy, dating from 1909.

Landwaiters (who, like riding officers, came under the supervision of the land surveyor) were responsible for supervising the landing of cargo from foreign ports, and securing it until all duties had been paid. Coastwaiters performed similar duties with vessels engaged in the extensive coastal trade, which was often used as a cover for smuggling. Even before a ship touched land, it would have been boarded by tidewaiters (also called tidesmen); their task was to ensure that the vessel did not make an illicit landing of dutiable goods before it tied up at the quay. By the 1780s there were *c.* 550 tidewaiters in the London service alone, and they accompanied every ship, in either direction, between Gravesend in Kent and London. While ships engaged in foreign trade were required by law to trade through officially designated ports, coastal traders might use smaller quays or harbours, referred to as 'creeks'. Here the Customs service might station a rowing boat

Clovelly was one of
a number of small
harbours on the
north Devon coast
where smugglers
were active. The last
recorded seizure of
a vessel there was
in 1825.

Opened in 1828,
St Katharine Docks
in London provided
robust protection
against pilfering
and smuggling.
Cargo could be
loaded almost
directly into bonded
warehouses under
the supervision of
customs officers.
It was only released
when duty had been
paid.

with four or five oarsmen, supervised by a boatsitter, who sat in the stern
and took command. They kept an eye on the coast for which the outport was
responsible, and had jurisdiction as far as the first bridge across any river in
their area.

Although tidesmen and boatmen were among the lowest-paid customs
officers, they had the opportunity to increase their income with prize
money for captured contraband. The work, however, was not without
danger, and tidesmen in particular risked being attacked. One of many who

succumbed to this fate was William May, a tidewaiter stationed at Portsmouth, Hampshire. In December 1749 he boarded the sloop *Charming Peggy*, then in Portsmouth harbour. In the course of trying to prevent two casks of brandy being whisked ashore in a wherry, he was struck on the head by a seaman, William Kemp, and thrown overboard. May drowned, and his body was never recovered. With no police force to collect evidence and prosecute, the Customs service had to do this work itself. Although the commissioners were adamant that a case should be brought, the only reliable witness, another tidesman named John Forrest, had been 'in Liquor' at the time, and was at first unclear as to the precise course of events. An affidavit was eventually secured from him, and Kemp was sent for trial at the Winchester assizes. He was found guilty, was hanged on Southsea beach, and his body was then hung in chains.

There can be no doubt that many customs men were 'in Liquor' while on duty, and little doubt that many were corrupt and connived with smuggling. R. S. Hawker, though not always the most reliable witness, wrote a short piece entitled 'The Gauger's Pocket', which originally appeared in *Household Words* in 1853. In it he recounted a story told to him by Tristram Pentire, 'the last of the smugglers', who was taken on by Hawker as general servant. The Gauger's Pocket of the title was a secret hiding place, where bribes would be left for the preventive officer. If, when greeted with 'Sir, your pocket is unbuttoned', the customs man replied 'Ay! Ay! But never mind, my man, my money's safe enough', it was a signal that the bribe had been accepted and a landing could be made without interference.

By the end of the eighteenth century it would have been a mammoth task for the ordinary citizen to navigate his or her way through the mass of customs legislation that then existed. The laws had never been consolidated, and the commissioners and senior officers at the Custom House in

When seized, smuggling vessels were sawn up and sold by the Customs. It appears that they were sometimes used to make roofs for huts or even cottages.

Dated December 6, 1836.

✓ **PORT OF PENZANCE.**

By Order of the Honourable Commissioners of His Majesty's Customs.

ON TUESDAY the 20th of December, 1836, at Eleven o'Clock in the Forenoon, will be exposed to PUBLIC SALE at the Custom House, at this Port, 2¾lbs. TEA, ONE NORWAY BATTEN, also, the Broken-up HULL of the Schooner "SUSAN," of St. Ives, seized and condemned for having been employed in Smuggling, together with the SAILS, ROPES, MASTS, YARDS, and all the other MATERIALS belong to the said Vessel.

Also, FOUR unserviceable Coast-Guard BOATS, and sundry Spars, Hawsers, Cordage, and other Stores, from Revenue Cruisers and Coast-Guard Stations.

The Goods may be viewed at the Custom House, on the day preceding the day of Sale.

Custom-House, Penzance, Dec. 2, 1836.

Notice of the sale of the broken-up hull of the smuggling schooner *Susan* at Penzance Custom House in 1836.

ANNO QUADRAGESIMO SEPTIMO

GEORGII III. REGIS.

Seſſ. 2.

CAP. LXVI.

An Act to make more effectual Proviſion for the Prevention of Smuggling. [13th Auguſt 1807.]

WHEREAS it is expedient to make further Regulations for the more effectual Prevention of Smuggling, and of the illegal Importation of Goods, Wares, and Merchandize; be it therefore enacted by the King's moſt Excellent Majeſty, by and with the Advice and Conſent of the Lords Spiritual and Temporal, and Commons, in this preſent Parliament aſſembled, and by the Authority of the ſame, That from and after the paſſing of this Act, every Veſſel belonging in the Whole or in Part to His Majeſty's Subjects, or whereof One Half of the Perſons on board ſhall be Subjects of His Majeſty, exceeding the Burthen of Fifty Tons by Admeaſurement, which ſhall be rigged or fitted as a Lugger, ſhall, together with her Guns, Furniture, Ammunition, Tackle, and Apparel, be forfeited, and ſhall and may be ſeized by any Officer of His Majeſty's Army or Navy or Marines, or of Cuſtoms or Excise.

II. Provided always, and be it further enacted, That the Owner or Owners of every Veſſel or Boat, rigged and fitted at the Time of the paſſing of this Act, not exceeding the Burthen of Fifty Tons by Admeaſurement, who ſhall be deſirous of navigating ſuch Ship or Veſſel, for the Purpoſe of fiſhing or carrying on lawful Trade, or as a Packet, or for any other lawful Purpoſe, ſhall take out a Licence from the Commiſſioners of the Cuſtoms in England, Scotland, or Ireland, or any Three or more of them, within Two Months after the paſſing of this Act; and during ſuch Period of Two Months from the paſſing of this Act, no ſuch Veſſel

500 Pounds REWARD.

Whitehall, January 10, 1828.

WHEREAS it has been humbly represented to the KING, that in the Night of Thursday, the 3rd Instant, a large Party of Smugglers, to the number of upwards of Two Hundred, armed with Fire Arms and other offensive Weapons, feloniously assembled on the Sea Shore at GALLEY HILL, near BEXHILL, in the County of SUSSEX, and were aiding and assisting in the illegal landing, running, and carrying away of uncustomed Goods; that in opposing this felonious Act, and in seizing part of the said Goods, CHARLES COLLINS, a First Rate Quarter Master of His Majesty's Ship HYPERION, was killed, and others of the said Ship wounded; and that upon an Inquisition held on the body of the said Charles Collins the Jury have returned a Verdict of "Wilful Murder against Persons unknown."

HIS MAJESTY for the better discovering the Persons who have been guilty of this Felony and Murder, is hereby pleased to promise HIS MOST GRACIOUS PARDON to any one or more of the Persons so assembled (except those who actually committed violence on the said Charles Collins, or any of the Officers or Men of the HYPERION, as shall discover his Accomplices, so that they may be apprehended and brought to Justice.

LANSDOWNE.

AND HIS ROYAL HIGHNESS the LORD HIGH ADMIRAL is pleased to direct that a Reward of

FIVE HUNDRED POUNDS

shall be paid and distributed to and amongst any Persons (except as aforesaid) who shall give such Information to CAPTAIN MINGAYE, or any of the Officers of the HYPERION, as shall lead to the Discovery, Apprehension, and Conviction of the said Offenders; such Reward to be paid by Mr. CHARLES JONES, the Solicitor of the Admiralty and Navy, on Conviction of the said Offenders, or any of them.

J. W. CROKER.

London had to refer to twenty large volumes of relevant statutes. These were not available to the public. A commissioner wrote in 1784:

The computation has become so intricate and extensive, that there are very few people who understand the business properly, nor is it easy to procure assistance … the duties are so complicated that it is hardly possible for a general merchant to know what duties he may be liable to pay. (Smith, G. 1980, pp. 74–5)

The laws did not just relate to duties and administrative matters, but included ever more hysterical attempts to stamp out smuggling and to bring the perpetrators to justice. The Smuggling Act of 1721 made convicted smugglers liable to transportation (removal to a penal colony) for seven years. In 1736 the same penalty was applied to smugglers resisting arrest (if unarmed); the death penalty applied to those wounding or taking up arms against an officer.

An Act of 1746 imposed the death penalty on those who assembled for the running or landing of contraband, or who blackened their faces or wore a mask or other disguise. Killing a customs officer meant that gibbeting would follow hanging. Notorious smugglers were to have their names advertised in the *London Gazette*. Failure to hand themselves in within forty days made them liable as outlaws, while those who harboured or hid gazetted men were subject to the death penalty. Collective punishment could also be imposed on whole communities for aiding smugglers, and heavy financial penalties were imposed. The carrot as well as the stick was employed. The same Act offered a reward of £500 to anyone who secured the arrest of a gazetted person. Attempts were also made to persuade smugglers to turn King's evidence. A piece of legislation passed in 1736, the Act of Indemnity for Smugglers, laid down that any smuggler could obtain a free pardon for past offences, as long as he disclosed them fully and named his associates.

It took a brave man to inform against his fellows, for in doing so he placed himself in danger of a revenge killing. Brutal treatment was meted out to suspected informers. Tight security was required to get an informant safely to the courtroom to give his evidence, and protection was sometimes given afterwards. A notorious case was that of Roger Toms, a crew member of the smuggling vessel the *Lottery*. In December 1798 she was surprised running contraband ashore near Cawsand in Cornwall. Shots were fired, and the boatman of the Cawsand customs boat was shot and instantly killed. The smuggling vessel cut her cable and escaped, but was taken some months

Opposite:
A poster of 1828 offering a reward for information leading to the capture of those responsible for the death of Charles Collins, First Rate Quarter Master of HMS *Hyperion*, a frigate stationed on the Sussex coast between 1825 and 1831 as part of the coastal blockade.

A revenue cutter chasing a lugger, *c.* 1830. The cutter is flying 'revenue stripes,' a legal requirement when giving chase.

King's Lynn Custom House was built between 1684 and 1685, and originally served as a merchant exchange. It was acquired by the Crown in 1718 and used by the Customs until 1989. The Norfolk and Suffolk coasts were much used by smugglers.

later by the revenue cutter HMS *Hind*, which took the *Lottery* (and such of her crew as had not escaped) into Plymouth. Under questioning, Toms named the man he said had fired the fatal shot. As the key witness, Toms had to be kept on the *Hind* until the other smugglers had been placed in custody. Even then his wife had to keep him hidden from his former associates, some of whom were still at large. However, it was to no avail. She was persuaded by them to give him up, and Toms was spirited away to Guernsey, a notorious centre for smuggling. His presence there was discovered and, despite difficult issues of sovereignty between the islanders and the English authorities, he was brought back. Under military escort Toms was taken to London, where he

CUSTOM-HOUSE, LONDON,
14th December, 1814.

WHEREAS it has been represented to the Commissioners of His Majesty's Customs, that on the night of the 7th instant, JOHN SMITH, Commander of the HIND Cutter, in the service of the Customs, and his Crew, when about to take possession of a Smuggling Vessel in the Harbour of Meragissey in the County of Cornwall, were feloniously assaulted and obstructed by a large body of Smugglers, armed with Fire Arms and other offensive Weapons, who fired upon the said John Smith and his Crew, and succeeded in conveying the Smuggled Goods on board the said Vessel, on shore.

The Commissioners of His Majesty's Customs, in order to bring to Justice any one or more of the said Offenders, are hereby pleased to offer a REWARD of

TWO HUNDRED POUNDS

to any Person or Persons who will discover and apprehend, or cause to be discovered and apprehended, the said Offenders, to be paid by the Collector of His Majesty's Customs at the Port of *Falmouth*, upon conviction.

By Order of the Commissioners,
GEORGE DELAVAUD,
SECRETARY

A notice in the *Royal Cornwall Gazette* offering a substantial reward for information leading to the apprehension of those who fired on the commander and crew of the revenue cutter *Hind* in 1814.

Poole Custom House in Dorset was burnt to the ground in 1813, and rebuilt in its present form the same year. It was strategically placed mid-way along the Town Quay, allowing observation of all approaching ships once they had rounded Brownsea Island.

Engraved for The Malefactor's Register.

Dodd delin.   *Page sculp.*

A PIRATE *hanged at Execution Dock.*

gave his evidence. The man against whom he testified was found guilty of murder and was hanged. Toms still did not gain his freedom. He could never have returned to his home in Polperro, and as his evidence might still be needed against men still at large, he was lodged at Newgate. He was given a job as an under-turnkey (or jailor), and he remained there, effectively a prisoner, until his death.

Although the prosecuting authorities relied on the evidence of informers, it was not always the case that this was sufficient to secure a conviction. Defence counsel tried to show that a man who would betray his companions to save his own skin, as well as for financial gain, was not to be relied upon. Juries would often agree. Indeed, it was very hard to secure juries that would bring in a conviction for smuggling. During the passage of the Smuggling Bill in 1736, it was claimed that 'in some parts of the maritime counties the whole people are so generally engaged in smuggling that it is impossible to find a jury that will, upon trial, do justice to an officer of the revenue in any case whatever'. The speaker went on to say that in the case of alleged smugglers killed by revenue officers in the course of an affray, coroner's juries frequently brought in a verdict of murder, ignoring pleas of self-defence. In such cases, if the officer was subsequently found guilty of murder it was common for the death sentence to be waived. While a reluctance to convict those charged with smuggling and related offences in part may have reflected sympathy with smuggling, in which many people had a greater or lesser interest, in the minds of many jurors the threat of retaliation would also have been lurking.

Magistrates, too, might be intimidated. An account, published in 1749, of the brutal murder of a customs officer and an informer in Sussex observed that 'If any [smuggler] happened to be taken, and the proof ever so clear against him, no magistrate in the country durst commit him to gaol; if he did he was sure to have his house or barns set on fire, or some other mischief done him, if he was happy to escape with his life.' In high profile cases such as this, the reluctance of local people to assist in the prosecution of the law could be circumvented in two ways. Firstly, the accused might be sent for trial in London or some assize town away from the locality where the offence took place. Alternatively, a Special Commission could be established, with assize judges sent out from London. Security would be high, both in transferring prisoners to jail and while they were lodged there awaiting trial. Members of the notorious Hawkhurst Gang in Kent were rescued from Newgate prison before their trial began, and it was not uncommon for dragoons to be called in to aid the civil power.

If it was difficult to obtain convictions against smugglers, the desire to deter others from offending was expressed by the severity of punishment for those found guilty. The eighteenth century was a brutal age; by its close there were over 200 offences that carried the death penalty, although the sentence was often commuted. Some 35,000 death sentences were handed down in England and Wales between 1780 and 1830, but only 7,000 were carried out. For the unlucky ones, public execution (which was not abolished until 1868) was intended as a final humiliation, though, all too often it took on a party atmosphere and became a public celebration. Only the poor, of course, went to the gallows. The middle- and upper-class consumers of smuggled goods went unpunished.

Opposite: The hanging (c. 1795) of a pirate at Execution Dock by the River Thames, at Wapping. A number of smugglers were also executed at this site, their bodies later being hung in chains from a gibbet. At public executions the cry 'Hats off!' was not intended as an act of respect, but rather to enable those at the back of the crowd better to see the spectacle.

An anatomical cast of the flayed body of a man, intended to show the musculature. Such écorché figures were produced from a cadaver, usually that of an executed criminal. Although there is some controversy over the identity of this particular individual, it is known that he was executed at Tyburn, London, in 1776. The choice is between James Langar (a footpad, or highwayman), and Benjamin Harley and Thomas Henman (who were both smugglers). The name that has long been given to this cast – Smugglerius – lends weight to one of the latter pair. Gibbeting and dissection were employed to add further horror and humiliation to a public hanging.

29

A PRACTICAL GUIDE
TO SMUGGLING

A NUMBER of historians have referred to 'the smuggling industry'. This description appears to lend a certain legitimacy to the activity, as though smuggling might be compared with the iron industry or the textile industry, or any other industry one might think of. The phrase does, however, link with what is now called the 'black economy' – activity which may involve vast sums of money and absorb the labour of hundreds or thousands of people, but which is hidden from the authorities' view.

While a body of evidence exists about failed smugglers, the successful ones left little or no trace of their activities. For this reason, estimates of the extent of smuggling must be treated with great caution. However, attempts have been made to quantify smuggling and its impact. In 1750 it was estimated that 3 million pounds (in weight) of tea were smuggled annually – more than three times the legal trade. A commentator in 1783 put the amount of tea illegally brought in as 11 million pounds (in weight), and reckoned (though on what basis is unclear) that 60,000 men were engaged in smuggling. Figures of seizures have greater credibility. In February 1825 the *Royal Cornwall Gazette* quoted an account published by the House of Commons of seizures by all the preventive services over the previous three years. This included 902,684¼ pounds of tobacco; 227,000 gallons of gin; 135,000 gallons of brandy; 19,000 pounds of tea; and 10,500 gallons of whisky. Incongruously, the list also included 'a single musical snuff box'. These seizures produced £287,541, or roughly one eighth of the cost of securing them.

Although smuggling ventures varied in scale, it is quite clear that the largest ones faced issues with which many law-abiding entrepreneurs were familiar. These included establishing sources of supply for the goods traded; the financing of the purchases; the capital costs of bringing the goods in (principally the cost of a smuggling vessel); and landing and distribution, including finding the best markets.

Opposite:
Smugglers surprised.
This print is one
of a pair, the other
being on page 42.
A smuggler loads
his pistol, while
another hurriedly
hides a tub of spirits
beneath a trap in
the floorboards.

As smuggling was known all around the coast of Britain, foreign supply towns tended to vary according to the location of the smugglers' home bases. Those along the southern coast of England inevitably depended on ports on the opposite side of the English Channel. Flushing, Ostend and Dunkirk were particularly important for locally produced gin, while warehouses in Calais, Boulogne, Dieppe, Le Havre and Cherbourg were also important. Many of these places had British expatriate communities to provide services for the smuggler.

Some West Country smugglers bought their brandy direct from Nantes, though it was more usual for them to purchase from intermediaries in the Channel Islands. These islands have a long history of semi-autonomy; to this day they are not considered part of the United Kingdom, but are Crown Dependencies. Although British customs officers were based on the islands from 1767, effective customs control was not established until 1805. As a consequence, much illicit trade moved to the ports of Roscoff and Saint-Malo in Brittany.

The Scilly Isles lie about 28 miles off Land's End, and in the eighteenth century it was said that scarcely anything was carried on there other than smuggling. Pilot gigs went out to intercept homecoming merchant ships, from which the smugglers purchased dutiable goods that were then sold on to smugglers from Cornwall and Devon. The coasts of the Bristol Channel and the Irish Sea were also supplied from offshore islands, especially Lundy and the Isle of Man, the latter also servicing Wales, north-east England and south-east Scotland.

Many transactions for the purchase of goods to be smuggled into Britain took place at sea. Continental suppliers of spirits and other items on which duty was payable in Britain would sometimes purchase their own ships and bring them to within a few miles of the English coast, where they acted as

In this nineteenth-century engraving of Kynance Rocks, Cornwall, a fisherman appears to have found a tub washed up on the beach. Harsh punishments were often imposed by smugglers on anyone who did not hand over such booty to them.

floating warehouses. Small boats (often fishing vessels) would set out to meet them and make purchases; they then returned to England, where they attempted to land their contraband. The government tried hard to curb the practice. In 1718 the first of a number of 'hovering acts' was passed. It was enacted that any vessel of fifty tons or under laden with tea, brandy or French silks that was found hovering within two leagues (about six miles) off the coast was liable to seizure.

The problem was still in evidence over a century and a half later, although the quality of the goods traded appears to have deteriorated greatly. In 1882 a convention was agreed between the British, Dutch and German governments, designed finally to stamp out the supply ships; at that time they were referred to as coopers (pronounced 'copers'), a name

deriving from the Low German *kôper*, meaning trader or dealer. They were described in an official report of the time as 'floating grog-shops [which] chiefly hail from German and Dutch ports.... They trade in tobacco and spirits of vile quality ... and latterly in immoral and obscene cards and photographs.'

Smugglers also did business at sea with regular merchant ships, including those of the East India Company. Masters and crew frequently engaged in a little private enterprise on the side, although the consequences could be

Gin Lane, a print by William Hogarth issued in 1751, depicting the debilitating effect on the populace of gin drinking. The scene is set in the St Giles district in London, in which a quarter of all residences in 1750 were gin shops. Above the doorway in the bottom left corner is the well-known saying 'Drunk for a Penny. Dead drunk for two pence.'

The struggle between preventive officers and smugglers sometimes resulted in violent skirmishes involving large numbers of men, leaving many dead and wounded.

serious if they were caught. Among the goods traded were tobacco from America, and tea and fabrics from the Far East. There was a profusion of sought-after fabrics from India, including both silks and cottons; muslins and 'chints' (chintz) were popular, but other types – including bejutapauts, cuttanees, carridarries and niccanees – are now likely to be recognised only by experts in textiles and historic costume. The running of contraband from legitimate trading vessels is often underplayed, with officers and crew attempting to bring ashore goods that were not included in the cargo manifest. Legitimate trade provided good cover. For example, in July 1817 the *Royal Cornwall Gazette* reported the case of a French vessel, which was a frequent visitor to Portsmouth. Ostensibly, its trading aim was to deliver eggs and fruit, but its actual aim was to bring in smuggled silk gloves, to buy stolen copper and other material from the dockyard, and to pass forged banknotes.

Smuggling, like any other trade, required capital. Ships had to be acquired, contraband articles had to be regularly purchased, and there were other expenses to be met. It was certainly the case in the West Country, and possible elsewhere, that groups of workers came together to form syndicates to finance smuggling. More often, though, the smugglers turned to wealthier individuals to provide funds. Members of the local gentry, prosperous farmers or merchants might be approached to put up capital. The utmost discretion would be promised, and anonymity would be respected.

Although most of the wealthy individuals who financed smuggling have escaped the attention of history, the exploits of some are known. One such was Thomas Benson. Born into a wealthy north Devon family, he built up a smuggling base on the island of Lundy. Many of these financial backers were pillars of their communities, and had no direct interest in the goods involved; others, such as some merchants and traders, saw smuggling as a means of expanding the stock in which they dealt. Sheep farmers in Kent and Sussex might secure a double dividend; the owlers would sell their wool on the Continent, and use the proceeds to bring back a cargo of contraband. It seems clear that the middlemen made most profit and took least risk. It is true that they might lose their investment, and it has been suggested that, to prevent this, the violent smuggling gangs of Kent and Sussex were encouraged. However, it was unlikely that the men behind the scenes would end up in prison or swing from the gallows.

In the early years of the eighteenth century smuggling deals appear to have been settled in cash, but in later decades sophisticated banking arrangements were employed. A vivid insight is afforded by William Hickey, for many years a successful attorney in India. In 1770, on a homeward journey aboard the East Indiaman *Plassey*, the ship was boarded off the Lizard in Cornwall by a smuggler who had come to trade. After negotiating a price for a large quantity of tea, the ship's captain and the smuggler proceeded to settle up:

[the smuggler] took from his pocket book a check, which, filled up for twelve hundred and twenty four pounds, he signed and delivered to the Captain. I observed it was drawn upon Walpole and Company, Bankers in Lombard Street.

Hickey later asked the Captain if he felt secure in accepting a cheque for such a large amount, to which the officer replied: 'These people always deal with the strictest honour. If they did not their business would cease.'

Zephaniah Job, who lived in Polperro between about 1770 and 1822, was known as 'the Smugglers' banker', and was personally engaged in both smuggling and privateering. The historian Martin Wilcox has suggested that his epithet somewhat diminishes the breadth of his activities, for as well as being a smuggler he was a farmer, a merchant, a provider of financial and legal services, a government contractor and a banker who started his own cheque-issuing country bank.

Whether acquired from an overseas port or from a ship at sea, contraband goods had to be brought back to Britain and landed covertly on her shores. Both at sea and on land, concealment was of the greatest importance. Many smuggling vessels were designed and constructed by shipbuilders with the express intent of increasing their speed and providing places of concealment. False bulkheads might be fitted within the ship, or even a false bottom or bow. The *Asp* of Rye was one such ship. She was seized in 1822 and found to have a false bow, access to which was by two scuttles (small openings), one on each side of the stem. Space was provided for no fewer than fifty flat tubs of spirits besides dry goods. Contraband might also be hidden beneath ballast or bulky cargo.

The topsail schooner *Pride of Baltimore II*, pictured off the island of Lundy in the Bristol Channel. In 1748 Thomas Benson, who was both MP for Barnstaple and a wealthy merchant, acquired the lease of Lundy, which he fortified and used as a smuggling base. He was reviled for allowing the captain of one of his ships to go to the gallows, after the vessel had been destroyed in an insurance fraud. Benson died in Portugal in 1771.

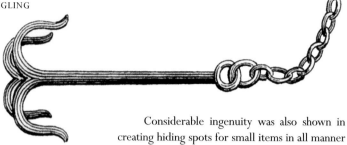

Some smugglers 'sowed a crop' by sinking a line of tubs offshore for later retrieval. In an attempt to catch any sinking-ropes, preventive men would tow a grapnel of 'creeper' along the seabed. Creeping was part of the regular duties of revenue officers, seeking to find tubs before the smugglers did.

A painting by an unknown artist, c. 1800, of mounted troops engaging with smugglers on a narrow beach. Some smugglers appear to be escaping in a galley, while others are being chased off in the left foreground.

Considerable ingenuity was also shown in creating hiding spots for small items in all manner of places, either in the vessel itself or concealed in otherwise legitimate cargo. At different times watches were found hidden in cheap imported French shoes, and silk gloves inside wooden toys. Bottles of whisky were discovered stuffed inside oven-ready turkeys, and tobacco was packed to look like hams. In December 1844 the *Hampshire Advertiser* reported that customs officers at Plymouth had examined the *Zebra*, a sailing packet from Jersey. They found thirteen casks said to contain pitch. Feeling that they were too light for that, they examined the casks more carefully. They found that there was indeed some pitch in them, but they had been fitted with tins containing a total of fourteen or fifteen hundredweight of tobacco.

Casks of spirits were among the bulkiest items smuggled, and were difficult to hide. Before the preventive services became more active at the end of the Napoleonic Wars, the common cask was the anker. Each of these contained about eight and a half gallons, a quantity easily carried on horseback. When men became the principal carriers, the half-anker (containing a little over four gallons) became more common. During a landing, the smuggling

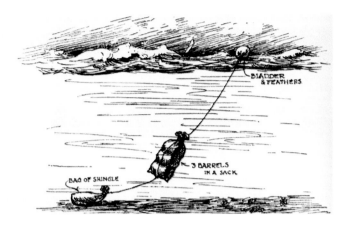

A device employed by smugglers at Sandwich, Kent, in the 1820s. A sack containing three half-ankers of spirits was attached to a line, on the end of which was a 30-pound bag of shingle acting as a sinker. The tubs floated just below the surface of the water. To aid retrieval, an inflated bladder and a bunch of feathers marked the spot.

A splendid hand-painted signboard lists the holidays observed at the Southampton Custom House in 1807. In addition to all Sundays, the Customs enjoyed a total of forty-four holidays a year – all of them good times to land smuggled goods.

37

Jumping Jenny landing her cargo. This hand-coloured aquatint is similar in composition to many depictions of contraband being landed. In reality, smugglers avoided moonlit nights, which made their activities too visible.

vessel either had to run on to a suitable beach to unload, or else lie offshore and transfer the casks into smaller tub-boats in order to bring them ashore. Each of these practices took time, and left the smugglers' ship very vulnerable. The practice therefore developed of weighting the tubs with sinking stones and attaching a line of them to a tub (acting as a buoy) either on or just below the surface. This was known as 'sowing a crop'. Most smuggling craft had a rail (known as the tub-rail) that ran the length of the hull on the inboard side. The line of tubs, with their sinking stones already attached, could be fixed to this rail by short lashings. Cutting the lashing meant that the whole line of tubs would drop into the sea, to be collected later. They could not be left indefinitely, or their contents would spoil. Even then, when treated with herbs and other material, the tainted spirits could be sold; this was known in the West Country as 'stinkibus' or 'stinky-booze'.

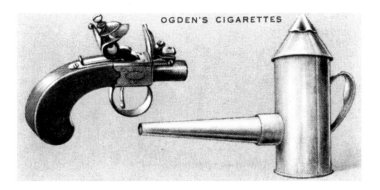

The flash pistol, sometimes known as a flink, and the spout lantern were used by smugglers to send signals at night. The spout lantern worked on a principle similar to that of the dark lantern used by Victorian policemen: by twisting the cap, a beam of light could be directed down the spout. Its narrow beam could be seen by ships at sea, but was difficult to detect by customs men ashore.

Whether sneaking into a harbour or running onto a beach, making a landing left smugglers at their most vulnerable. Landing contraband was very much a combined operation, involving the smugglers at sea and those on shore. It was the landsmen who took the initiative, and who ran the greater risk. The 'master smugglers' took the larger part of the profit, and many of them quickly amassed a considerable fortune. No doubt the risks involved also account for the landsmen's having the reputation of being the most violent of all the smuggling fraternity.

The operation was fraught with uncertainty. Last-minute decisions had to be made about the precise location to be chosen as the landing site, depending on the weather and upon the known whereabouts of the preventive men. Although many paintings depict smugglers toiling beneath the light of a full moon, it was a situation to be avoided if at all possible, as detection was made easier. Paradoxically, some customs men were given two nights off before and after full moon, as this was such a quiet time for smuggling activity. Every effort was made to confuse the authorities as to the precise location of a landing, and to entice customs men away from the chosen spot. Newspaper reports of the time give numerous accounts of the devices employed. The *Royal Cornwall Gazette* recorded two audacious episodes within a couple of months of each other in 1826. In August a man feigned drowning at Dover to divert preventive men, whereupon smugglers made off with casks down the thronging Marine Parade. In November a smuggling ship anchored off Cromer, and enticed preventive officers aboard. These were then taken prisoner, while the smugglers' crop of casks was put ashore. The preventive men were then put back in their rowing boat, but with all the oars smashed so that pursuit was impossible.

The logistical problem was to bring all elements of the operation together at the same time and in the same place. For a substantial cargo this meant horses and carts, as well as men to act as porters or as strong-arm men to defend the others. The porters who carried spirits were known as

Although this Sussex 'batman', wearing his farm smock, may appear benign, he was anything but. These men, armed with stout clubs which they were not afraid to use, were the strong-arm men who protected the smugglers when a landing was made, or when contraband was being transported inland.

tubmen; they carried a tub on their chest and one on their back, the two slung together with straps or ropes. Together these could weigh 70–100 pounds (31–45 kg), and the pressure on chest and back made breathing difficult. Tubmen were expected to move at a fast pace and often had to walk for miles inland; spinal damage was common among them.

Communication between ship and shore was difficult in the extreme, and the Smuggling Act of 1807 made any kind of signalling illegal. A person was made liable to a fine of £100, or up to one year in prison with hard labour, if they should

make or assist in making, or be present for the Purpose of assisting in making, any Light, Fire, Flash, or Blaze, or any Signal by Smoke, or by Rocket, Firework, Flags, Firing of Guns, or other Fire Arms, or any other

Moonrakers is a nickname attached to residents of Wiltshire. The story goes that some yokels were surprised by preventive men one moonlit night as they used rakes to retrieve tubs from a pond. Asked what they were doing, they replied that they were trying to collect the 'cheese' that was floating on the water. Faced with such apparent madness, the preventive men went on their way.

Contrivance in or on board or from any Ship, Vessel, or Boat, or on or from any Part of the Coast of Great Britain, or within Six Miles thereof, for the purpose of giving any Signal to any Person on board of any Smuggling Vessel or Boat.

It did not matter if the signal could not be seen or heard from the ship, nor even that there might be no ship actually hovering at all.

The 'professional' smugglers often lacked the resources to handle a large shipment on their own, and were dependent on the assistance of others for labour, and for the provision of horses and sometimes carts or wagons. In November 1744 the Collector of Customs at Eastbourne reported that between 500 and 600 horses were present in Pevensey Bay moving contraband from three cutters. In September 1783 around 300 men on horseback were present at a landing at Cuckmere, with between 200 and 300 again present a week later. These armies of men, either willing or coerced, could be brought together with amazing speed; the Hawkhurst Gang, for example, claimed to be able to gather 500 armed men together within one hour.

The landing party had to shift contraband goods away or into hiding as quickly as possible. Around 1815, smugglers at Deal in Kent constructed permanent pits on the beach at nearby Sand Hills. These were about four feet deep, lined with planks and covered by a trough filled with shingle.

A painting, dated 1792, attributed to George Morland. On a rocky shore men are unloading tubs from the boat that has brought them from the smugglers' vessels lying offshore. A wagon waits to carry them away. Such paintings satisfied a great appetite for images of the romantic and the exciting.

Captain M'Culloch of HMS *Ganymede*, serving in the coast blockade, reported that smugglers 'were enabled to remove their cargoes into them in a few minutes'.

Other convenient places were used to hide contraband for a short time, and these certainly included caves. That does not mean that every cave on every beach around the shores of Britain was a smugglers' cave, although the fascination with smugglers and a love of hide-and-seek would have it so. The same caution is needed with houses and other buildings near the coast. When houses were put up by a builder without the aid of an architect, and when they were expanded in a piecemeal way over time, it was inevitable that there should be odd nooks and crannies; today these can be viewed as having a significance that is not merited. Nor is there anything intrinsically odd about houses having cellars, or underground storage areas entered through a trap door. However, farmhouses and cottages *were* used as temporary hiding places, although the house owner often agreed under duress. It was a brave (or reckless) farmer who refused to harbour a few tubs on his premises, or refused to allow his horses or carts to be used, or his workers to be employed.

Contraband goods were of no value to the smuggler while they were hidden away. As soon as it was considered safe to do so, they had to be moved on to those willing to pay cash for them. These included private clients who were known to purchase smuggled goods, and, indeed, may have supported the smugglers in other ways. Establishment figures, including members of Parliament and clergymen, are known to have belonged to this group. The Reverend James Woodforde, rector of Weston Longville in Norfolk at the end of the eighteenth century, recorded in his diary numerous deliveries of smuggled goods. On 29 March 1777 he wrote:

> Andrews the Smuggler brought me this Night about 11 o'clock a Bagg of Hyson Tea 6 Pd Weight, He frightened us a little by whistling under the Parlour Window just as we were going to bed. I gave him some Geneva and paid him for the Tea at 10/6 Per Pd – [£] 3. 3. 0

Tradespeople (including tea dealers) also had to be supplied. To give an air of legitimacy, traders often bought some stock on which the full duty had been paid, for this provided cover for the contraband items. The smugglers would head for the nearest market town to dispose of their booty. In some places this was easier said than done. West Cornwall, an area renowned for smuggling, was particularly isolated in the mid eighteenth century. The mother of the famous chemist Sir Humphrey Davy wrote that when she was a girl, 'West Cornwall was without roads, there was only one cart in the town of Penzance, and packhorses were in use in all the country districts.'

Opposite:
A nineteenth-century aquatint of smugglers being attacked by revenue men. This is one of a pair, the other being on page 31.

The tunnel leading to Ness Cove at Shaldon, Devon. Frequently described as an 'original smugglers' tunnel', this description appears to be far from accurate. A likelier (but more prosaic) explanation for the tunnel is that it was constructed in the 1860s, at the order of Lord Clifford, to facilitate access to Ness Cove from Shaldon village.

In 1754 *The Gentleman's Magazine* observed that what served as roads in the district were mere bridle paths, 'remaining as the deluge left them and dangerous to travel over'.

Elsewhere, smugglers made use of ancient tracks, green lanes and drovers' roads. The coastline of eastern England has many rivers and inlets that enabled contraband to be brought inland in small boats. Kent and Sussex had the advantage of proximity to London, together with many roads leading to the metropolis. Although the commissioners of customs frowned on random 'stop and search', local officers often needed reminding of the fact. Pusey Brooke, the Customs Surveyor-General of Hampshire and Dorset, wrote to his subordinates at Portsmouth on 27 June 1748:

The demand from a prosperous local town for smuggled luxury goods such as lace and silk was a boon to smugglers. Brighton (or Brighthelmston) served such a function for Sussex smugglers, especially after the fashion for sea bathing developed and the Prince Regent began to patronise the place. Although contraband is known to have been landed directly in the town, the beaches at nearby Hove were far more suitable. This 1864 illustration is from *Jeff's Guide to the Royal Pavilion*.

[You] are not upon any Account whatsoever to search Coaches and Waggons without a positive Information to which Directions you are to show yourselves strictly Obedient, the same being given in pursuance of an Order from the Board dated the 22d April 1735.

London was the great magnet, with the suburban village of Stockwell in Lambeth the London depot for smugglers from the southern counties. It was said mid-century that smugglers 'came to London about two or three in the morning, and could sell to particular dealers from 1,000 to 2,000 pounds-weight [of tea], and be out of town again by six in the morning; and, by this quick return, they generally made a voyage every ten days'.

A drawing from a Coastguard officer's journal of May 1834 illustrates a method used by six young men smuggling tea from Calais. The officer stated that it was 'so well arranged that the most correct eye could not discover the deception'.

Smugglers used all manner of green lanes, tracks and paths to convey the contraband inland from a landing site. This track, a known smugglers' trail, leads towards Vereley Hill in the New Forest, Hampshire.

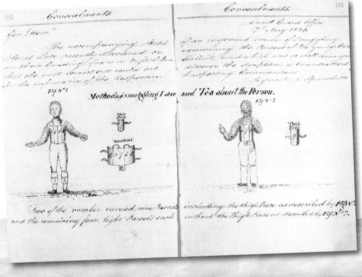

THE SMUGGLER AT SEA

In 1671 the Board of Commissioners of Customs was established by Charles II. The first line of defence against the smuggler was on the sea itself, and from the 1670s the Board of Customs hired small sloops and smacks (fishing boats) to watch out for owlers. In 1698 the board acquired its own sloops to patrol the coast. Yet by 1703 there were only eight revenue vessels patrolling from the Bristol Channel to the North Foreland in Kent, although these continued to be supplemented by ships provided by private contractors.

At this time smugglers tended to use small vessels, much like those employed in the fishing industry (as many of them were), and these were fitted with a lug sail and sometimes a gaff sail. With this type of rig, the mast is set well forward, close to the bow, and the spar carrying the sail is attached to the mast at a point about a third along its length. As it hangs diagonally, the spar rises higher than the mast, enabling the vessel to carry a larger spread of canvas. In the case of a gaff rig, the spar supporting the lug sail is attached at one end to the mast. These fore-and-aft rigged vessels were highly manoeuvrable, and, being able to tack into the wind, could enter or leave a harbour or creek much more easily and swiftly. The smaller craft also had a shallower draught, which admirably suited them to inshore work.

In the course of the eighteenth century many of the larger smuggling operators had their vessels custom-built. The cost, which might be around £2,000 for a large ship, could be covered by making as few as four successful voyages. To gain the maximum speed the ships were carvel-

The revenue cutter HMS *Chameleon*, painted in 1856 when on duty off the Sussex coast. A feature of revenue cutters was their long, fixed bowsprit, which was sometimes almost as long as the hull. This unique feature, which increased the vessel's speed, was prohibited on all other vessels by an Act of 1787.

built, with the boards of the hull butting up to each other, rather than overlapping as in clinker-built vessels. To cut costs, fir might be used rather than oak. In the event of capture a less valuable craft would be forfeit, although in practice the increased lightness of fir-built ships increased their speed, making capture less likely. Shipbuilders proved adept at constructing ships for smugglers that stayed inside the law but gained maximum advantage by stretching the legal restrictions to the limit. In May 1837 the *Bristol Mercury* noted that when Pitt the Younger introduced legislation laying down permitted measurements for galleys (another popular smuggling vessel), the 'plan forbidden was so good a plan, that the smugglers at once adopted it as a model, and had their boats constructed in the French ports precisely according to the measurements prohibited'. The paper recorded Deal boatmen as saying that 'they never knew [how] to build a boat for smuggling till Billy Pitt taught them the way'.

Harvey's shipyard, Littlehampton, West Sussex. It was not unknown for shipyards to build boats for the preventive services as well as for smugglers. In consequence, there was much cross-fertilisation of design and construction between the two kinds of vessel.

Experience showed that smuggling ships often had a competitive edge over the revenue vessels. Not only did they excel in speed and manoeuvrability, but also their crews often outclassed those of the government ships when it came to seamanship. In his *Naval History of Britain, 1783–1822*, Edward Brenton noted that Cornish smugglers

> are as remarkable for their skill in seamanship as for their audacity in the hour of danger. Their local knowledge has been highly advantageous to the Navy, into which, however, they never enter, unless sent on board ships of war as a punishment for some crime, committed against the Revenue Laws. They are hardy, sober, and faithful to each other, beyond the generality of seamen. (White, 1997)

The outcome of an engagement between a revenue vessel and a smuggler's lugger could never be taken for granted, for the latter were often well armed, mounting perhaps fifteen four-pounder cannon and having the equivalent of 'marines' to fend off boarding parties. The greater the penalties that legislation threw at smugglers, the greater their incentive to fight, and they often acted with great audacity. In 1777 the Board of Customs was sent a report from one of its officers of a large lugger off the coast. This vessel was so well armed that she was considered 'greatly an overmatch' for even

A mid-eighteenth century trade card for Parkinson, tea dealer. The description 'from Twining's' may indicate the source of the tea. Richard Twining, a son of the firm's founder, was frequently consulted by Prime Minister William Pitt, whose Commutation Act of 1784 reduced tea duties from 100 to 25 per cent, which had a great impact on smuggling.

Parkinson,
from Twining's
TEA DEALER & GROCER
at the three Golden Sugar Loaves,
in Rupert Street
Near the Hay Market
LONDON.

In the *Hampshire Advertiser* of 19 May 1838, J. J. Wolff lets it be known that he can supply everything that a sea captain (no doubt including a smuggler) might need to protect his vessel. He includes cannon and ammunition as well as 'Small Arms of every description'. It was not until the Firearms Act of 1920 that general gun control was introduced into Britain.

J. J. WOLFF,
FROM THE ROYAL ARSENAL, WOOLWICH.
BEGS to inform the Owners and Build-
ers of YACHTS, MERCHANT and TRADING
VESSELS, that he has constantly on sale at his shop,
77. HIGH STREET, SOUTHAMPTON,
nine, six, four, three, two, one, and half pounder
BRASS and IRON CANNON and CARRONADES
mounted on sea service carriages complete. Also, all
sorts of Ammunition ; Small Arms of every description ;
brass staunchions, yokes, rullocks, belaying pins, spi-
ders for yachts' masts, tomahawks, boarding pikes, signal
lanthorns, Kingston and cabin lamps, prismatic and
other deck lights, charts, nautical books, quadrants,
compasses, binnacles, telescopes, log and time glasses,
blue lights, rockets, and fireworks of every description,
with directions for firing.
A very powerful L be for sale; also, one 7-inch
centre ditto, cast iron ed and cylinder poppet; also,
one small 3-inch centre ditto.
Cat gut and couplings for bands.
Old Brass Cannon b ught and taken in exchange.
A good assortment of best cutlery and fishing tackle.
AN APPRENTICE WANTED.

two revenue cruisers or sloops. So highly regarded were the smuggling luggers that, if seized, they might be taken into the public service instead of being broken up.

Strict protocols applied in a sea chase. By law, revenue vessels were required to hoist the revenue colours and fire a gun as a signal (usually, but not always, with a blank round) before opening fire on any smuggling vessel. Furthermore, if it seemed likely that a seizure was about to be made, it was necessary for an officer on the revenue vessel to take cross-bearings to fix his ship's position precisely. If out of sight of land, he would reckon the number of leagues the ship had run since the last bearing had been taken. Without this information, vouched for by a second officer, it was easier for a smuggler, when brought to court, to claim that he had been outside the prohibited limits.

Patrolling the coast as a deterrent to smugglers was costly, and, in an attempt to increase efficiency, responsibility was transferred over time from one body to another. In the 1780s the size and armament of revenue cutters was increased, as were their overall numbers. Smugglers responded by sinking rafts of tubs offshore for later recovery (sowing a crop). As the revenue cutters became bigger, smuggling craft tended to become smaller. These craft were cheaper to construct and had a better turn of speed. Smugglers also employed gigs – open rowing boats propelled by up to twenty oarsmen, greatly in excess of the legal limit of six oars imposed on all rowing boats by an Act of Parliament in 1721. Such boats could race across the Channel with considerable speed. Much later, in May 1832, the commander of the Lowestoft Coastguard was reported in the *Essex Standard* as having captured, on a tributary of the River Blackwater, 'a beautiful eight-oared smuggling boat', with her entire cargo, consisting of 164 tubs of brandy and 120 packages of dry goods. The crew managed to escape.

During the long war with France, the activities of British smugglers were actively encouraged by the French government. They were given free access to all the Channel ports, and part of the port of Dunkirk was set aside for them. Following the financial crisis of 1789, the French government was in great need of English gold. It was estimated that about £10,000 in gold coins was being smuggled out of England each week, without which the wages of French troops might not have been paid. Smugglers also took British newspapers and other intelligence over to France. Not all smugglers should be tarred with the brush of treachery, however. Information about French plans was brought back to England, while many smugglers used their intimate knowledge of the French coast to act as pilots for Royal Navy expeditions.

In 1809 a new force called the Preventive Waterguard was established. This body was intended to operate in coastal waters, linking up with the riding officers on land and the customs cruisers that operated further out to sea. The Waterguard manned watch towers set up along the coast; these served to accommodate the men, who were deliberately stationed away from their homes and families in order to reduce the risk of collusion with the smugglers. The men were required to row nightly patrols along the stretch of coast for which they were responsible. If bad weather made this impossible, they were to patrol the coast on foot, on the lookout for likely landing places.

James Gillray's satirical print of 1795 is a reminder that smuggling sometimes consists of illegally sending goods *out* of a country. During the wars against France, smugglers were charged with trading British produce and goods (including arms) across the Channel. The sacks of flour in the bottom left-hand corner are destined for Dieppe and Ostend.

The end of the war against Napoleon in 1815 brought problems of its own. Thousands of discharged soldiers and sailors had to be reintegrated into civilian society. The navy was to be reduced from nearly 150,000 to fewer than 20,000. Both officers and men were affected. Many discharged seamen and soldiers had acquired a taste for action and a disinclination for a quiet life; for many others, unemployment loomed large. In such circumstances smuggling might have seemed an attractive proposition. Some officers tried to get by on their half-pay, and some entered foreign navies. Others sought employment in the Customs service.

In 1816 control of the revenue cutters was passed to the Admiralty, although the Board of Customs continued to bear the cost. In the following year a total 'coast blockade' was set up along the Kent coast between the North Foreland and Dungeness. A year later the blockade was extended to Seaford in Sussex. The Waterguard, considered by many to be an ill-disciplined force, was withdrawn from this area, but continued elsewhere. In 1822 it was renamed the Coast Guard (later

Under legislation passed in the reign of George III, any seaman on a vessel caught smuggling could immediately be impressed into the Royal Navy for five years. Their seafaring skills were highly regarded. The law was not repealed until 1834.

A painting by Thomas Butterworth (1768–1842) of a smuggler being chased by a brig. Butterworth was invalided out of the Royal Navy in 1800, and soon afterwards was appointed as a marine painter to the East India Company.

merged into the single word Coastguard). The coast blockade was not without its failings, and it tended to attract the dregs rather than the cream of the lower decks. However, these roughs were, perhaps, just the men to break up the smuggling gangs, especially when brought under the discipline of their commander, Captain Joseph M. McCulloch, RN, known in naval circles as 'Flogging Joey'. McCulloch's success was such that the coast blockade was not disbanded until 1831, when it was transferred to the national coast guard.

By the 1830s the nature of smuggling was changing. In his tale *The Three Cutters*, published in 1836, Captain Frederick Marryat wrote: 'Smugglers do not arm now – the service is too dangerous; they effect their purpose by cunning, not by force.' Engagements between revenue cutters and smuggling vessels continued to be reported, as did beach affrays, but they became less frequent. Cannon and cutlass gave way to concealment, with steamships offering fresh hiding places, more difficult and dangerous for customs officers to rummage. What might be considered the 'heroic' (or brutal) age of smuggling was undoubtedly passing. Smuggling, however, was not dead; it simply moved to a new phase.

In the period after the Napoleonic Wars some officers discharged from the navy were willing to enter the Coastal Blockade service as midshipmen, a rank hitherto accorded to young men training for a commission. They were based on shore and received a midshipman's pay of around £36 a year.

A British man-of-war in pursuit of a sailing lugger – a painting (c. 1825) from the circle of Thomas Butterworth. Although flying the skull and crossbones, the vessel being chased is likely to be engaged in smuggling rather than piracy.

William Galley, brought cross a Horse to a Sand Pit where a deep Hole is Dug to Bury him in.

The unfortunate William Galley put by the Smugglers into the Ground & as is generally believed before he was quite DEAD.

SMUGGLERS OF NOTE
AND NOTORIETY

İT SHOULD COME as no surprise that while there were thousands of
smugglers in the eighteenth and nineteenth centuries, we know the
identities of very few. Of those that we can identify, our knowledge is often
limited to a name or, more frustratingly, merely a nickname. Black Tooth,
Bulverhythe Tom, Flushing Jack, Little Fat Back, Nasty Face, Old Joll, One-
Eye, Will the Fiddler and Yorkshire George all had their part to play in the
history of smuggling, even if we know next to nothing about them.

The majority of information that we have about smugglers comes from
those who were set against them. Those who had the misfortune to be
caught at least secured a place in history, although the historian has to drag
through legal and administrative documents to find them. The more
notorious sometimes ended up at the Old Bailey and are easier to bring to
light, as many of the records of that court are available online. Thus we learn
of John Catt, hanged at Tyburn in March 1741. Catt had been sentenced in
1737 to seven years' transportation to Virginia for smuggling, but had
returned before completing the sentence and promptly took up his old ways
again. All last words from the scaffold have to be treated with caution, but
Catt appeared to show no remorse for his behaviour:

> We now begun to grow so daring, that it was thought necessary to reinforce
> the Officers with more Men, in order to put a Stop to our Proceedings; but
> we having Intelligence, had recourse to Fraud, and so still managed our
> Matters very well. I cannot help taking Notice here, that we thought
> ourselves in no unjustifiable Actions, tho' unlawful ones, and I was so
> unhappy as to imagine, that our Crimes we were committing every Day,
> was not contrary to the Laws of Reason and Nature, tho' to those of Man.
> (*The Proceedings of the Old Bailey, 1674–1913*)

Most smugglers were likely to have been illiterate or barely literate at best,
and thus did not write autobiographies or memoirs. One who did was the

Opposite:
The body of William
Galley, a murdered
customs man, was
not discovered until
several months
after his death. He
had been cruelly
mutilated and
reputedly buried
while still alive.

To the Memory of
ROBERT TROTMAN
*Late of Rond in the County
of Wilts,* who was barbaroufly
Murder'd on the Shore near
Poole the 24 March 1765

Alittle Tea one leaf I did not fteal
For Guiltlefs Blood fhed I to GOD appeal
Put Tea in one scale human Blood in tother
And think what tis to flay thy harmlefs Brother

Graves commemorating smugglers are more common than one might imagine, and may reflect a certain local respect for men who were seen to stand out against the established orders. Robert Trotman was shot while assisting in a landing near Poole, and was buried in the village churchyard at Kinson, now incorporated into Bournemouth.

aforementioned Harry Carter, a member of the Carter family based at Prussia Cove in Mount's Bay, Cornwall. From this cove Harry and his brothers John and Charles ran a profitable smuggling enterprise between 1770 and 1807. John had a reputation as an honest smuggler. He once broke into the Penzance Custom House to retrieve confiscated tea that was secured there. He claimed that he was required to get the tea back because he had promised to deliver it to his customers by a certain date, and needed to protect his business reputation. However, he was at pains to take nothing but that which he considered to be rightfully his.

Harry Carter wrote a memoir that was first published in the *Methodist Magazine* in 1831, after he had given up smuggling and taken up Methodism. He eventually became a lay preacher. Harry took up smuggling at the age of twenty-five, and soon commissioned his own 18-ton sloop, eventually trading up to a 60-ton cutter. 'I went on for many years sinning and repenting,' he wrote. In 1777 he was arrested in Saint-Malo on suspicion of piracy, having no papers about him. After his release in 1779, as part of a prisoner exchange, he returned to smuggling, operating heavily armed cutters based in Guernsey. In 1787 he was seriously wounded while trying to land contraband at Cawsand on the River Tamar. After hiding for three months, he escaped to Italy, and then moved on to America. It was here that

Prussia Cove, just east of Cudden Point, Mount's Bay, Cornwall. This was the lair of the Carter family, noted West Country smugglers.

he was gradually drawn into Methodism, and the book becomes an account of his gradual spiritual awakening. Some readers have found this tedious, but without it the book would probably not have been written, for it has been established that a large number of autobiographies written by people with working-class origins (Carter's father was a tin miner) were written as testimony to the change brought about in their lives by religion.

In marked contrast to Carter's account is *Memoirs of a Smuggler*, published in 1837 and containing 'The principal events in the life of John Rattenbury, of Beer, Devonshire; commonly called "The Rob Roy of the West" '. Whereas Carter appears to have penned his own story, 'Jack' Rattenbury's account bears the marks of what we would now describe as a ghost writer. It reads like a Victorian 'Penny Dreadful', and is full of tales of derring-do, with much attention paid to daring escapes from the hand of the law.

English prisoners in France during the Napoleonic Wars – an engraving from Captain Marryat's novel *Poor Jack*, published in 1840. Many British people, including merchants and smugglers, were imprisoned by the French. Among them was Harry Carter, the noted Cornish smuggler who wrote about his experiences in his autobiography.

Rattenbury was born at Beer in 1778. His father was a shoemaker, but gave up his trade and, before Jack was born, went aboard a man-of-war, never to be heard of again. Jack took up fishing with an uncle, but soon abandoned this in favour of joining a privateer. Like Carter, he was captured by the French, and was imprisoned at Bordeaux. Making his escape, he found an American ship whose captain was willing to take him to New York. There he found another American vessel which took him to Copenhagen, and from there he made his way to Guernsey, before returning home to Beer. Jack found it impossible to settle there, and determined on a career in smuggling. He was taken by a press gang but eventually escaped while ashore, only to realise that he had left his pocket book on board the ship, with his name (he had been using an alias) and place of abode contained within it. He was now hunted as a deserter, and went back to sea on a privateer. His career from then on was a mixture of smuggling (with his own vessels), piloting and engagement in legitimate coasting trade. Like many other smugglers, he had a relaxed attitude towards patriotism.

John Rattenbury, a Devonshire smuggler. How widely he was known as 'The Rob Roy of the West' remains unclear. Sir Walter Scott's novel was published in 1817, some twenty years before Rattenbury's biography appeared.

He accepted £100 to take four French prisoners who had escaped from Tiverton jail out of the country, his excuse being that he thought they came from Jersey. However, he also agreed to pilot the *Linskill*, a transport ship carrying part of the 82nd Regiment of Foot through the dangerous Needles Passage off the Isle of Wight. It may have been this which gained him the patronage and protection of Lord Rolle, who secured for him a job on the revenue cutter *Tartar*, and eventually gave him a pension of 1s. a week when he fell on hard times. It is equally likely that Rolle was one of his customers for smuggled goods. Rattenbury was a restless character who lacked the piety which Carter eventually found, and who spent several spells in prison. Yet, despite his swashbuckling nature, he lacked the brutal streak that was to be found in many others. He died in 1844, at the age of sixty-five, and is buried in an unmarked grave in Seaton churchyard.

Rattenbury was far from being unique in standing on both sides of the law. A generation or two earlier, in neighbouring Cornwall, Isaac Cocart had been a two-timer – two times mayor of Falmouth, and both a magistrate and a smuggler. Convincing others that he had renounced his criminal ways, he was given command of the 43-ton customs sloop the *Prince of Cornwall*. His seizures appear to have been modest, but that was often the way with corrupt officials: provide *some* evidence that you were doing your job, and you might retain the cover of your position.

Cover was, of course, important to those who used their official position to further some illegal activity, but it was easy to blacken a person's reputation, and lack of evidence is sometimes taken as indicative of an individual's skill in concealing his guilt. This may be true of John Knill, who held the office of Collector of Customs at St Ives for twenty years from 1762. He was elected mayor in 1767, but in 1782 left the town to take up residence in London. It has been popularly supposed that Knill was a smuggler, but the evidence to support this is slight. He was certainly eccentric, a character trait which may have aroused suspicion. In the year that he left St Ives he erected a curious mausoleum on a hill outside the town, intending (so he said) to be interred there, but he was buried in London. The curious pyramidal structure led people to suggest that it was intended as a marker for his smuggling vessels. His eccentricity extended to his will, in which he left a sum of money to provide for ten virgins to dance round the obelisk every five years. They still do.

If the story of John Knill illustrates an attempt to attach a legend to a man, that of 'Cruel Coppinger' reflects the desire to find the man behind a legend. The story of Cruel Coppinger was first disseminated by the Reverend R. S. Hawker, another Cornish eccentric. It originally saw light in the magazine *All the Year Round* in December 1866, and was republished in Hawker's *Footprints of Former Men in Far Cornwall*. Hawker claimed that 'there was a ballad in existence within human memory which was founded on the history of this singular man'. The first verse ran:

Will you hear of the bold, brave Coppinger
How he came of a foreign kind?
He was brought to us by the salt water;
He'll be carried away by the wind.

On a stormy night, 'a strange vessel of foreign rig' was wrecked on the north Cornish coast. There was only one survivor, Coppinger, a

Gunsgreen House, Eyemouth, Berwickshire, built in 1753 for John and David Nisbet, local merchants and smugglers. In the eighteenth century Eyemouth was a centre of smuggling activity. The town has been described as the tunnelling capital of Britain. Whether the tunnels are all (or even mainly) smugglers' tunnels is uncertain.

Dorothy 'Dolly' Peel lived from 1782 to 1857 and was a resident of South Shields on the River Tyne, where this statue is to be found. She was a fishwife, a smuggler and a protector of seamen from the press gang. She was one of numerous women throughout the country who supported smuggling, often by hawking contraband goods.

'man of herculean height and mould'. Hawker continued:

He plunged over the bulwarks, and arose to sight buffeting the seas. With stalwart arm and powerful chest he made his way through the surf, rode manfully from billow to billow, until with a bound, he stood at last upright upon the sand, a fine stately semblance of one of the old Vikings of the northern seas.

Hawker asserted that Coppinger was a Dane, which adds to the drama, but this might also refer to the suggestion that one of the claimants to be the historic Cruel Coppinger came from a family that may, indeed, have had Danish roots. Having come ashore, Coppinger does not hang about. He immediately leaps upon a horse being ridden by a local heiress, Dinah Hamlyn, and soon persuades her to become his wife. There then follows a career of wrecking, theft and smuggling, accompanied by domestic violence and the terrorisation of the local populace, until Coppinger disappears in as theatrical a manner as he arrived.

Writing in 1909, C. G. Harper observed that the Coppinger story illustrated 'the growth of wild stories out of meagre facts'. The facts of the case are, indeed, few; furthermore, they are inconsistent. There was a Daniel Herbert Coppinger who married Ann Hamlyn in 1793. He might at some time have been in the Royal Navy, but there is no evidence that he was a smuggler. Becoming bankrupt in 1802, he spent some time in jail and ended his days in Barnstaple. The second candidate is John Copinger (spelled with one p) who came from Ireland and, in the late eighteenth century, was a successful smugglers' merchant in Roscoff, Brittany. Escaping from France at the time of the Revolution, he settled at Trewhiddle, near St Austell – on the south Cornish coast rather than the north.

There is one more peculiarity of the Cruel Coppinger story, namely the vein of violence that runs through it. This does not seem to have been the West Country way with smugglers, although Cornish wreckers had that reputation. It is true that blood was shed, but for truly vicious behaviour, perpetrated by the most bloodthirsty gangs, we have to look further east along the English coast. In the eighteenth century, Kent and Sussex smugglers exhibited a lawlessness and violence that bears comparison with the Wild West in America. Gangs of desperadoes, sometimes working together and at other times in competition, held much of the countryside in thrall. In April 1747 the villagers of Goudhurst (in what appears to have been a unique example of resistance to smuggling gangs) fought a pitched battle against members of the Hawkhurst Gang. The villagers dug trenches and placed men with firearms on rooftops and in the church tower. When the previously announced attack occurred, the Goudhurst men killed or wounded a third of the smugglers, and the remainder beat a hasty retreat.

A portrait of John Copinger, one of the candidates to be the real person behind the legendary 'Cruel Coppinger'. The Reverend R. S. Hawker who popularised the story is known to have been cavalier with facts.

Violence was integral to the activities of the smuggling gangs. It kept the revenue men at bay (with even the dragoons being cautious in their encounters with them), it secured labour and other logistical support, and it silenced witnesses. One of the reasons why smuggling took on this aspect particularly in Kent and Sussex may have been the proximity to London. The scale of the metropolitan market made it attractive to smuggling gangs, whose members also mixed with the London criminal underworld. The statements of condemned men on the scaffold frequently drew attention to their role in highway robbery, housebreaking and theft, with smuggling often representing the pinnacle of their criminal careers. Only a few seemed

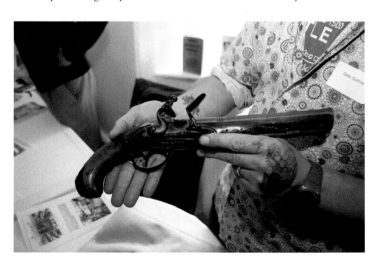

Smuggling artefacts with a clear provenance are rare. This adds greatly to the interest of this pistol, which is unquestionably a relic of the Hawkhurst Gang.

Opposite:
The smuggler
shown in this print
of 1830 by William
Heath is probably
a 'character', or
portrayal of an
actor. The somewhat
startled individual
is armed with a
cutlass and a brace
of pistols. He wears
heavy sea boots
and has an anchor
tattooed on his left
hand.

to have made a fortune. One who did was Arthur Gray of the Hawkhurst Gang. Starting out as an apprentice to a butcher, he was hanged (aged thirty-eight) at Tyburn in 1748, by which time he was alleged to be worth £10,000 (over £850,000 at today's values). Most seem to have been plebeian in origin, with mainly labourers and artisans appearing in the criminal records. The capitalists and middlemen behind the gangs – tea dealers, innkeepers and perhaps farmers – kept themselves in the background.

The extremes of violence perpetrated by the smuggling gangs is illustrated by the murders of Daniel Chater and William Galley in 1748. In September 1747, five months after the Goudhurst battle, the revenue cutter *Swift* seized the smuggling vessel *The Three Brothers*, and secured a substantial cargo of tea and brandy destined both for the Hawkhurst Gang and another gang based on the Hampshire border. The contraband was lodged in the Poole Custom House, although the smugglers themselves escaped in an

In this print, also
by William Heath,
a smuggler wears
his canvas petticoat
tucked in over
heavy sea boots, and
appears to have a
sou'wester on his
head.

British Smuggler

A Representation of ý Smugglers breaking open ý King's Custom House at **Poole.**

open boat. The local smugglers thought that the Custom House was too secure to raid (there was a navy sloop alongside the quay). However, stiffened by the resolve of the Hawkhurst men, a joint party broke in and retrieved the tea, though leaving the brandy. Using horses they had brought with them, the Hawkhurst Gang triumphantly carried their portion of the booty inland. As they passed through Fordingbridge, Daniel Chater, a shoemaker, happened to recognise Jack Diamond, one of the smugglers, with whom he had previously done harvest work. The two men chatted for a while and Diamond passed Chater a bag of tea, 'for old time's sake'. This was to prove the undoing of both men.

When a £200 reward was offered for information about the men who had broken into the Custom House, Chater came forward and informed on Diamond. It was necessary for Chater to be examined by a justice of the peace, and he was sent to Chichester for that purpose, escorted by William Galley (an elderly riding officer). They never arrived. Having stopped for rest and refreshment at the White Hart Inn, near Havant, the innkeeper realised their identity and informed the local smugglers. The two were liberally plied with drink until they became befuddled. The problem was what to do with them. When members of the Hawkhurst Gang arrived, it was decided that the captives had to be killed. They were severely beaten, tied to their horses and taken away, all the while being beaten with whips and sticks. Galley fell senseless from his horse, after which (having 'cut off his nose and his privities, [and] broke every joint in him') he was buried in a field. Chater suffered a similar fate and was tossed down a well, with stones thrown on top of him.

Even for such a brutal age, the savagery of these acts was shocking. The perpetrators were tracked down and seven were tried for murder and executed. Around the same time, others (including Thomas Kingsmill, the leader of the Hawkhurst Gang) were sentenced to death for their part in the raid on the Poole Custom House. The gangs were gradually broken up, although some lingered on into the 1820s. James Slingsby, reputedly 'the last of the Kentish smugglers', died in 1895 – in the workhouse.

The village of Rottingdean in Sussex had numerous smuggling connections. Around the year 1814, Whipping Post House was the home of 'Captain' Dunk, the village butcher as well as a smuggler.

HAM'S
Customs Year Book
1899.
A DIGEST
OF THE
LAWS & REGULATIONS OF H.M. CUSTOMS
(OTHER THAN THOSE RELATING TO WAREHOUSING, WHICH ARE DEALT WITH IN THE WAREHOUSING SUPPLEMENT),

TOGETHER WITH
DIRECTORY
TO THE
Ports, Harbours, and Bonded Warehouses
OF THE
UNITED KINGDOM,
INCLUDING THE
CUSTOMS ESTABLISHMENTS;

EDITED BY
E. GRANT HOOPER, F.I.C., F.C.S.,
VICTOR MASLIN,   WM. CRABTREE,
P. J. MAKEY,
OF H.M. REVENUE SERVICES.

LONDON
EFFINGHAM WILSON & CO., 11, ROYAL EXCHANGE, E.C.
1899.

FROM THE OLD SMUGGLER
TO THE NEW

THE SMUGGLERS of the eighteenth and early nineteenth centuries referred to themselves (and were often referred to by others) as 'the free traders', as though the imposition of duties on imported goods that the public desired was in breach of a basic freedom. It was this mindset that accounts for much of the public sympathy enjoyed by smugglers.

The government was in a bind: import duties made a vital contribution to the public revenues, yet at the same time the effort that went into the suppression of smuggling imposed an enormous expense. From at least the time of Adam Smith, many had argued that only a reduction of duties (or, better still, free trade) would remove the free traders' raison d'être. Yet it took eighty-four years from the appearance of Smith's *The Wealth of Nations* for free trade to reach its climax in 1860, with Gladstone's budget of that year and the Cobden–Chevalier Treaty with France. Debate had quickened after the Napoleonic Wars. Manufacturers (especially those of cotton textiles) became increasingly confident in their ability to compete in both domestic and foreign markets. At the same time, disruptions in trade brought about by the war against Napoleon, as well as the War of 1812 against the United States, increased pressure on the move towards freeing trade in the world markets. This lay behind the successful attack on the East India Company's monopoly in 1813, and a more liberal attitude to economic affairs by Tory governments in the 1820s. Although the number of commodities subject to duty was slashed, in the 1830s economic matters had to compete with vast social and constitutional questions for Parliamentary time. In 1840 mounting pressure for reform led to the setting up of the Select Committee on Import Duties, which was packed with free traders. In the words of the historian Lucy Brown, the committee's 'witnesses … were not so much examined as invited to give prepared propaganda lectures'. The committee demonstrated that out of a total customs' revenue of nearly £23 million in 1839, £21 million was raised on ten commodities; the remaining amount was raised by duties on 1,142 commodities, with some of these raising sums that were described as 'merely

Opposite:
Ham's Customs Year Book was issued between 1875 and 1930. It is a good source for those trying to trace particular customs officers.

The economist Adam Smith, as depicted by the Edinburgh caricaturist and engraver John Kay in 1790. Smith said of the smuggler that 'he would have been, in every respect, an excellent citizen had not the laws of his country made that a crime which nature never meant it to be'.

Passengers on vessels arriving from the Continent have their baggage examined at the Dover Custom House in about 1820. The increase in tourism in the nineteenth century meant that more effort had to be made to control smuggling, which in the individual case might be small in scale, but in total could add up to a considerable sum.

vexatious'. The first revision of the tariff was carried out in 1842, the second in 1845 and the third a year later. Within a short space of time over 1,200 articles were freed of duty.

The impact on smuggling was as profound as many had been arguing for decades. Although the practice did not cease, it diminished greatly and it changed in character. In May 1857 the *Royal Cornwall Gazette* reported that 'smuggling has greatly decreased. With the exception of those little piccadilos [sic] committed by "inconsiderate and unprincipled passengers," smuggling proper is now confined almost exclusively to tobacco, spirits, and watches.' The reference to 'smuggling proper' suggests that smuggling continued, but in a very different form; indeed, there is much evidence that this was the case.

Affrays on the beach and exciting sea chases became much rarer, and were seen as 'events' rather than regular occurrences. In December 1851 the *Royal Cornwall Gazette* reported a court case at Plymouth involving the smack *Wellington* of that port. She had been seized by the revenue cutter *Sylvia* off Padstow in Cornwall, after a chase in which about a hundred warning shots had been fired. Although the cargo of spirits had been destroyed to prevent seizure, ample evidence had been left behind, and tubs had been picked up in the sea when there had been no other ship within six miles. In July 1876 the *Exeter Flying Post* recounted the story of the Plymouth fishing boat *Dewdrop*,

which had been fired on by the revenue cutter *Spy*, resulting in one fisherman being shot in the back and shoulder by ball-cartridge. The commander of the cutter declared that, had the *Dewdrop* not hove to, he would have sent a six-pound shot at her. Although the incident was held to have been a 'melancholy blunder', it should be noted that the Isle of Wight was one of the last bastions of smuggling on a grand scale.

In the latter half of the nineteenth century the coasts of Britain, all of which had played host to smuggling, now became 'the seaside'. Increasing numbers of people sought access to the coast as holidaymakers, and the railways stimulated a middle-class taste for this. The middle classes valued respectability, and respectability clashed with the law-breaking activities

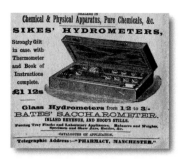

Benjamin Sikes won a competition of 1802 to design a new hydrometer, used to determine the strength of spirits, a measurement of crucial importance to both excise and customs officers. Between 1816 and 1907 this particular apparatus was the legal standard.

of smugglers, particularly those of the old smuggling gangs. Distance, however, in time as well as place, lends enchantment, and in the course of a few decades smuggling tales (whether true or fictitious) added a bit of spice to many a resort, or attractive beach, or cove. Smuggling came to attract the interest of the folklorist and the antiquarian, and fact and fiction became firmly entwined. The *Royal Cornwall Gazette* captured this interest in an article published on 14 June 1900:

CAMBORNE NATURAL HISTORY SOCIETY

On Thursday afternoon members of the above society paid a pleasant visit to Prussia Cove, the scene of many smuggling adventures in bye-gone days. Beneath the cliffs and near the mouths of the caves which were formerly used by the smugglers in their efforts to defraud the revenue, the pilgrims sat around on the rocks, while Mr. Howard Harris, of Porthleven, related many curious and interesting facts connected with smuggling days and smuggling ways. Tea having been partaken of, members of the party were greatly interested in visiting no less a person than the grandson of the once-famous "King of Prussia." This august and venerable personage, for he boasts some eighty-three summers, was in his summer quarters, but he was evidently proud of his ancestry, fond of relating his reminiscences, and of exhibiting his curios, which were indeed well worth seeing.

A smuggling ploy with which many an eighteenth- or nineteenth-century smuggler would have been familiar. In January 1994 HM Customs and Excise seized 1,250 kg of cocaine hidden in forty-seven drums of bitumen on board the cargo ship *Jurata*. Suspicions were aroused because the freight charges exceeded the value of the alleged contents. The cocaine had a street value of £250 million.

The new smugglers tended to be passengers trying to slip something past customs, or else crew members bringing back something for their family or to sell on the black market. As early as 1846 the Collector of Customs at Southampton reported that 'the extent of smuggling by the steamers was most extensive', and by 1867 the customs commissioners were reporting that smuggling by passengers and crew comprised the majority of cases. As noted previously, steamships provided crews with fresh opportunities for concealing contraband, either in the coal bunkers or hidden among the machinery. The protective casings around paddle wheels were a popular place, for these were difficult and dangerous areas for customs men to access. To counter this new threat, the revenue authorities introduced steam vessels of their own. The first was the *Vulcan*, launched as early as 1835.

Smuggling continues to this day, although the key locations may have changed – to the container port of Felixstowe, or Heathrow and other airports, for example. The preventive forces since 2009 have been men and women of the Border Force (an agency of the Home Office) rather than customs men. The trade of the smuggler now includes drugs, endangered species and people – though tobacco (in the form of cigarettes) is still a major item. There is one big difference with the past – the smugglers are not seen as either romantic or heroic. Yet.

Luggage from a boat train awaiting examination by customs officers at Charing Cross Station, London c. 1906.

FURTHER READING

An Alphabetical Abridgement of the Laws for the Prevention of Smuggling. Eyre and Strahan, 1818.

Baring-Gould, Sabine. *Devonshire Characters and Strange Events.* The Bodley Head, 1908.

Bathurst, Bella. *The Wreckers.* Harper Perennial, 2006.

Beck, John. *A History of the Falmouth Post Office Packet Service 1689–1850.* South West Maritime History Society, 2009.

Carter, Harry. *The Autobiography of a Cornish Smuggler.* Gibbings & Co., 1900.

Chatterton, E. Keble. *The Fine Art of Smuggling: King's Cutters vs Smugglers, 1700–1855.* J. B. Lippincott, 1912.

Defoe, Daniel. *A Tour Through the Whole Island of Great Britain.* Penguin, 1971.

Hampson, Geoffery (ed.). *Portsmouth Customs Letter Books, 1748–1750.* Hampshire County Council, 1994.

Harper, Charles. *The Smugglers: Picturesque Chapters in the Story of an Ancient Craft.* Chapman & Hall, 1909.

Hawker, Robert Stephen. *The Prose Works of Rev R. S. Hawker, Including Footprints of Former Men in Far Cornwall.* John Lane, 1903.

Hay, Douglas et al. *Albion's Fatal Tree: Crime and Society in Eighteenth-Century England.* Penguin, 1977.

Holmes, Neil. *The Lawless Coast: Smuggling, Anarchy and Murder in North Norfolk in the 1780s.* Larks Press, 2008.

J. J. R. *John Knill, 1733–1811.* Cunnack, 1871.

Leather, John. *The Salty Shore: The Story of the River Blackwater.* Seafarer Books, 2003.

Marryat, Captain Frederick. *The Pirate, and The Three Cutters.* Nonsuch Publishing, 2006 (first published 1836).

Morley, Geoffrey. *Smuggling in Hampshire and Dorset 1700–1850.* Countryside Books, 1983.

Parker, Derek. *The West Country and the Sea.* Longman, 1980.

Phillipson, David. *Smuggling: A History 1700–1970.* David & Charles, 1973.

Platt, Richard. *Smuggling in the British Isles: A History.* The History Press, 2011.

Pocock, Tom. *Captain Marryat: Seaman, Writer and Adventurer.* Chatham Publishing, 2000.

Proceedings of the Old Bailey, 1674–1913 (www.oldbaileyonline.org).

Rattenbury, John. *Memoirs of a Smuggler, Compiled from his Diary and Journal.* J. Harvey, 1837.

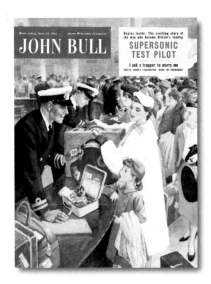

In this cover illustration from *John Bull* from September 1955, a decidedly nonchalant young passenger undergoes a customs examination at the dockside. By this date much of the effort to collect duties and prevent smuggling was centred on airports. Even so, the title of 'waterguard' applied to all uniformed customs officers until 1972.

Rule, John. *Albion's people: English Society 1714–1815*. Longman, 1992.

—— *The Vital Century: England's Developing Economy, 1714–1815*. Longman, 1992

Smith, Gavin D. *The Scottish Smuggler*. Birlinn, 2003.

Smith, Graham. *Something to Declare: 1000 Years of the Customs and Excise*. Chambers Harrap, 1980.

Tregarthen, J. C. *John Penrose. A Romance of the Land's End*. Cornwall Editions, 2004 (first published 1923).

Waugh, Mary. *Smuggling in Devon and Cornwall 1700–1850*. Countryside Books, 1991.

—— *Smuggling in Kent and Sussex 1700–1840*. Countryside Books, 1985 (revised edition, 1998).

Wesley, John. *'A Word to a Smuggler'* in *The Works of the Rev John Wesley, A.M.* (7 vols.), vol. 2. T. Mason and G. Lane, 1840.

White, Paul. *The Cornish Smuggling Industry*. Tor Mark Press, 1997.

Wilcox, Martin. 'Maritime Business in Eighteenth-Century Cornwall: Zephaniah Job of Polperro.' *TROZE*: The Online Journal of the National Maritime Museum, Cornwall (September 2010).

Woodforde, Reverend James. *The Diary of a Country Parson 1758–1802*. The Canterbury Press, 2011 (first published 1924–31).

PLACES TO VISIT

There are few museums devoted exclusively to smuggling. The two books by Mary Waugh, cited in the *Further reading* section, contain useful lists of places to visit, giving clear directions to beaches and other sites. A good gazetteer is Keith Wheatley's *National Maritime Museum Guide to Maritime Britain* (Caxton Publishing, 2000). Readers are advised to check opening times before visiting.

Deal Maritime and Local History Museum. 22 St George's Road, Deal, Kent CT14 6PA. Telephone: 01304 381344. Website: www.dealmuseum.co.uk

Gunsgreen House. Gunsgreen Quay, Eyemouth, East Berwickshire TD14 5SD. Telephone: 01890 752062. Website: www.gunsgreenhouse.org

Jamaica Inn. Bolventor, Launceston, Cornwall PL15 7TS. Telephone: 01566 86250. Website: www.jamaicainn.co.uk

Like smuggling, the retrieval of goods and material from wrecked ships was regarded by many people (especially those who lived from hand to mouth along the coast) as acceptable behaviour. Similar views prevail among some people in modern times. This illustration shows the beach at Branscombe, Devon, after the container ship MSC *Napoli* was beached in January 2007.

Lancaster Custom House, a fine Georgian building on St George's Quay, was built between 1763 and 1764 to the design of Robert Gillow, a member of the famed furniture-making family. It remained in use by customs until 1882. It now houses a maritime museum.

Lancaster Maritime Museum. Custom House, St George's Quay, Lancaster, Lancashire LA1 1RB. Telephone: 01524 382264. Website: www.new. lancashire.gov.uk/leisure-and-culture/museums/lancaster-maritime-museum.aspx

Merseyside Maritime Museum. Albert Dock, Liverpool Waterfront, Liverpool L3 4AQ. Telephone: 0151 478 4499. Website: www.liverpoolmuseums. org.uk/maritime (The museum houses the national collection of the UK Border Agency and Customs.)

The Museum of Smuggling History. The Undercliffe Drive, Ventnor, Isle of Wight PO38 1UL. Telephone: 01983 853677.

National Maritime Museum Cornwall. Discovery Quay, Falmouth, Cornwall TR11 3QY. Telephone: 01326 313388. Website: www.nmmc.co.uk

Old Town Hall Museum. High Street, Old Town, Hastings, East Sussex TN34 3EW. Telephone: 01424 451052. Website: www.hmag.org.uk

Polperro Heritage Museum of Smuggling and Fishing. Harbour Studio, The Warren, Polperro, Cornwall PL13 2RB. Telephone: 01503 272423. Website: www.polperro.org/museum.html

Rye Castle Museum. 3 East Street, Rye, East Sussex TN31 7JY. Telephone: 01797 226728. Website: www.ryemuseum.co.uk

INDEX